SOUND ADVANTAGE
A Pronunciation Book

Stacy A. Hagen
Edmonds Community College
Intensive ESL Program

Patricia E. Grogan
University of Washington
Intensive English Program

with technical illustrations by Schlomann Graphic Design
with cartoons by Dick Lande

PRENTICE HALL REGENTS, Englewood Cliffs, New Jersey 07632

Library of Congress Cataloging-in-Publication Data

Hagen, Stacy A.
    Sound advantage : a pronunciation book / Stacy A. Hagen, Patricia
  E. Grogan ; with illustrations by Schlomann Graphic Design ;
  with cartoons by Dick Lande
        p. cm.
    "Companion text to Sound advice: a basis for listening"—Pref.
    ISBN 0–13–816190–9
    1. English language—Pronunciation.   2. English language—
  Textbooks for foreign speakers.   I. Grogan, Patricia E.
  II. Title.
  [PE1137.H27   1992]
  421'.54—dc20   91–23275
                                                     CIP

Acquisitions editor: Anne Riddick
Editorial/production supervision and
   interior design: Tara Powers-Hausmann and E.A. Pauw
Cover design: Wanda Lubelska Design
Prepress buyer: Ray Keating
Manufacturing buyer: Lori Bulwin

© 1992 by Prentice Hall Regents
Prentice-Hall, Inc.
A Simon & Schuster Company
Englewood Cliffs, New Jersey 07632

Photo Credits

Page 86: Pete Vasquez, The Houston Post, Houston, TX. *Page 98:* Ken Karp. *Page 110:*
O.E.O. *Page 125:* Irene Springer. *Page 147:* Fred R. Bell, National Park Service. *Page 162:*
Marc P. Anderson. *Page 171:* Laimute E. Druskis. *Page 186:* U.S. Geological Survey,
Department of the Interior.

Printed in the United States of America

10   9   8

ISBN 0-13-816190-9

Prentice-Hall International (UK) Limited, *London*
Prentice-Hall of Australia Pty. Limited, *Sydney*
Prentice-Hall Canada Inc., *Toronto*
Prentice-Hall Hispanoamericana, S.A., *Mexico*
Prentice-Hall of India Private Limited, *New Delhi*
Prentice-Hall of Japan, Inc., *Tokyo*
Simon & Schuster Asia Pte. Ltd., *Singapore*
Editora Prentice-Hall do Brasil, Ltda., *Rio de Janeiro*

*For my family: Kim, Tori, Bob, and my
father, Robert; my grandparents, Florence
and Palmer.*

*   *   *

*For Marshall, who showed me how to
turn adversity and fear of the
unknown into challenge and
adventure.*

*For Naomi, an adventurer like her
father, who keeps me connected with
the wonders and joys of life.*

Contents

Preface ix
To the Teacher x
*Pronunciation Preview: A Guide to Using the
    Dictionary* xiii

1 Syllable Recognition and Reduction   1

Part I: Syllables 1
Part II: Stressed Syllables 2
Part III: Recognizing Syllable Stress in English 3
Part IV: Ellipsis 9
*Part V: Unstressed Syllables with Non-Reduced
    Vowels* 11

An Overview of English Vowels   15

2 Lax Vowels   18

Part I: /æ/ 18
Part II: /ɪ/ 22
Part III: /ɛ/ 26
Part IV: /a/ 30
Part V: /ʊ/ 35

3   The Tense Vowels   40

> *Part I: Diphthongs /ay/, /aw/, /oy/ 41*
> *Part II: /iy/ 45*
> *Part III: /ey/ 49*
> *Part IV: /uw/ 52*
> *Part V: /ow/ 56*

4   Troublesome Consonants   60

> *Part I: /s/ and /z/ 61*
> *Part II: th /θ/ and /ð/ 64*
> *Part III: /r/ and /l/ 66*
> *Part IV: Nonreleased Final Consonants 72*
> *Part V: Consonant Clusters 75*
> *Part VI: Consonant Combinations in Phrases and
>   Sentences 78*

5   Linking   79

> *Part I: Linking with Vowels 79*
> *Part II: Linking Identical Consonants 82*

6   Consonant Replacements   87

> *Part I: The Flap 87*
> *Part II: The Glottal Stop 89*
> *Part III: Can/Can't 90*
> *Part IV: Negative Contractions 93*

7   Common Reductions   99

> *Part I: Reductions with /h/ 99*
> *Part II: going to/want to/have to/has to 102*
> *Part III: of 104*
> *Part IV: and/or/for 106*

8   Sentence Rhythm   111

    Part I: Sentence Stress and Unstress 111
    Part II: Content and Function Words 115
    Part III: Stress Timing 120

9   Information Focus and Intonation   126

    Part I: Information Focus: The Basic Pattern 126
    Part II: Common Intonation Patterns 128
    Part III: Contrasting New Information 133
    Part IV: Intonation Patterns That Change the
       Meaning 136
    Part V: Lists 145

10   Inflectional Endings   148

    Part I: Past Tense (-ed) 148
    Part II: Plural/3rd Person "s" 153
    Part III: -teen/-ty 157

11   Reductions in Consonant Clusters   163

    Part I: sts/sks/th Deletion 163
    Part II: nt Reduction 165
    Part III: Assimilation 167

12   Contractions   172

    Part I: Contractions with "will" 172
    Part II: Contractions with the Verb "be" 175
    Part III: Contractions with "have," "has," "does,"
       "did" 177
    Part IV: Contractions with "would" and "had" 180

Appendix A: Consonant Practice   187

/b/ *and* /p/   /w/
/v/ *and* /f/   /y/
/d/ *and* /t/   /h/
/g/ *and* /k/   /m/
sh /ʃ/ *and zh* /ʒ/   /n/
ch /tʃ/ *and j* /dʒ/   /ŋ/

Appendix B: Minimal Pair Practice with Consonants   198

b/p   t/p   g/k
b/v   d/z   v/w
f/p   d/j   v/ð
f/v   d/r   v/z
f/h   θ/t   ch/j
f/θ   θ/sh   y/j
s/sh   θ/s   w/r
sh/ch   θ/ð   n/ŋ
sh/j   ð/d   n/l
t/d   ð/z

Appendix C: Minimal Pair Practice with Vowels   202

I/iy   ɛ/ə   æ/ə
ɛ/ey   æ/a   ə/ʊ
ɛ/æ   ə/a   ə/ow
ɛ/a   I/ey   ey/a
I/ɛ   I/ə   a/aw
ey/æ   a/ow

Appendix D: General Rules for Predicting Stress (with
Supplemental Practice)   205

Transcripts for Listening Exercises   211

Preface

Sound Advantage: A Pronunciation Book has been designed as a companion text to *Sound Advice: A Basis for Listening* (Prentice Hall, 1992). While *Sound Advice* focuses on receptive skills, *Sound Advantage* teaches pronunciation and includes those elements essential to *production*. Designed as a comprehensive pronunciation text, it contains many skills necessary for improved fluency. Linking, reduction, intonation, word and sentence stress, ellipsis, consonant replacements, and inflectional endings are a few of the areas that complement traditional vowel and consonant practice.

This text provides a generous variety of methods and activities for instructors to choose from. Listening practice is an integral part of each chapter, since pronunciation and listening are interdependent and mutually reinforcing. Each listening section is followed by a number of production exercises, ranging from controlled practice to more student-generated material. Traditional minimal pair lists for both consonants and vowels have also been included to provide instructors with material for creating exercises tailored to their specific group.

Students preparing for the SPEAK Test will find the chapter review exercises particularly relevant. Short presentations, picture descriptions, and paragraph readings are included in many chapters to give students practice in the types of tasks demanded on the SPEAK Test.

One of our goals has been to make this text accessible to all ESL instructors, whether they have taught pronunciation before or not. With this in mind, all sounds are accompanied by detailed descriptions of how to form each sound and by articulation drawings, where appropriate.

Increasingly, programs are recognizing the need for pronunciation training, and students are asking for help in making their English more intelligible. We have designed these materials with the intent that they will be useful to both you and your students. We welcome your feedback.

Stacy A. Hagen
Patricia E. Grogan

To the Teacher

Sound Advantage: A Pronunciation Book is designed for intermediate/high intermediate to advanced students. The topics can be successfully covered in one term; however, an instructor wishing to cover *all* exercises in all chapters may need a longer period of time.

Suggestions for Exercise Presentation

Pretests. Teachers will find these useful for diagnosing problem areas and deciding whether a particular section is applicable for their students.

Explanations. The box format allows for presentation of the material in a clear, concise manner. Teachers are encouraged to summarize the information for students, perhaps writing a few key ideas on the board.

Articulation Descriptions. These descriptions may be used as a resource for the teacher, as well as a method for talking students through the formation of the sound. J. C. Catford argues that since pronunciation is a motor skill, students must be taught "precisely what to do with their vocal organs."* He has found intensive silent introspection to be the most effective method, and we have incorporated aspects of this idea with the introduction of each new sound. Teachers may suggest that students close their eyes as they go through the description.

Listening. There are a variety of listening exercises:

> listening for two items that are the same or different
> listening for two items that are the same, and one different
> looking at three items and deciding which one has a different vowel sound

*Catford, J. (1987). Phonetics and the Teaching of Pronunciation: A Systematic Description of English Phonology. In J. Morely (ed). *Current Perspectives on Pronunciation.* Washington, D.C.: TESOL, p. 99.

filling in the blanks

listening for a particular feature

listening for and marking a particular aspect of pronunciation

In Chapters 2 and 3 (lax and tense vowels), the listening exercises are not limited to a single minimal pair contrast (e.g. "meet/ mitt" for the sound /iy/). Teachers will also see, for example, "meet/ met," or "meet/mutt." This allows instructors to choose the contrast(s) that are problematic for their students. Teachers who wish to target a particular minimal pair contrast will find the appendices in the back of the text useful for creating additional exercises.

Production Exercises.   Teachers can have students practice the words, phrases, and sentences in a variety of ways:

listen and repeat (individually, in pairs, or groups)

students pronounce, teacher pronounces, students pronounce (so that students can check their pronunciation against the teacher's)

finish the sentences with words of their choice

create sentences for other students to repeat based on words/ phrases they have practiced

create questions for other students to answer based on words/ phrases they have practiced

dictate words/phrases/sentences for other students and/or native speakers to write down

"whisper" or silently form a word/phrase to better feel the target feature(s)

exaggerate or slow down the articulation of the target feature to better feel it

All but the open-ended production exercises are on tape, so students can have the opportunity for as much individual practice as they like.

Chapter Review Exercises

Dialogues.   Suggested activities include the following:

listen and repeat (individually, in pairs, or groups)

listen for and mark particular features to prepare for pronouncing them

perform the dialogues in pairs or in front of the class while other students monitor speaker's pronunciation

Paragraph Readings.   This activity has been included to help pre-pare students for the SPEAK Test and to give students practice with discourse-level pronunciation. We suggest two approaches:

> students first read text to themselves for meaning, and mark potential pronunciation problems; then they listen and read aloud

> students first listen to paragraph read aloud and mark areas of difficulty; then they read aloud

Short Presentations.   These are included as preparation for the SPEAK Test and practice for extemporaneous speaking. Students study the information and present it in their own words. The teacher may want to encourage students to add information related to their own experience and background to make the talk more personal.

Picture Descriptions.   On the SPEAK Test, students are asked to either tell a story based on a series of pictures or answer questions about the picture.

In the exercises in this text, students can describe the picture, tell a story based on the picture, or ask other students questions based on the picture. The teacher may want to generate and go over key vocabulary first. See the Instructor's Manual for suggested questions.

Work with Native Speakers (Interviews, Dictations, Riddles).   Students are encouraged to have as much contact with native speakers as possible, and these exercises are designed with that in mind. We advocate ample practice in class to build students' proficiency and confidence before asking them to interact with native speakers.

A note about the vowel symbols: we generally follow the IPA (International Phonetic Association). In the case of the tense vowels and diphthongs, however, we have used the American Phonemic symbols because we wanted students to *see* the glides to /y/ or /w/.

*   *   *

An Instructor's Manual with chapter notes and supplementary material is available free of charge to all teachers. A set of four cassette tapes can be ordered from Prentice Hall Regents, Englewood Cliffs, New Jersey 07632, USA.

Pronunciation Preview: A Guide to Using the Dictionary

A Note to the Teacher: This section should be covered when you think it is appropriate for your students. Those with advanced language proficiency may be able to cover this material first; others with less advanced language skills may need to wait until the middle or possibly the end of the text.

To the Student: Most dictionaries will give you information on how to pronounce words. If you can learn to understand the pronunciation symbols that your dictionary uses, you will have a useful way to learn to pronounce words by yourself.

Part I: Information in Your Dictionary on Syllable Stress

Because syllable stress is so important in the pronunciation of English, dictionaries almost always show how many syllables a word has and which syllable gets the strongest stress. When you look up a word in the dictionary, it is important to pay special attention to this information.

beau·ti·ful

    (a) /byoo′tə-fəl/*

    (b) /ˈbyuᵂtəfəl/†

    (c) /ˈbyut-i-fəl/‡

a·long

    (d) /ə-lông′/*

    (e) /əˈlɔŋ/†

To show the strongest (primary) stress, an accent mark is placed either **after** the stressed syllable, as in (a) and (d), or **before** it, as in (b), (c), and (e).

ad·ver·tise

(f) /ˈædvərˌtaiz/‡

(g) /adˈvər-tīz'/*

(h) /ædˈvərtayz'/§

Many dictionaries also show which of the other, weaker syllables in a word have non-reduced vowels (often called *secondary* or *medium* stress). Such syllables are longer and stronger than syllables whose vowels are reduced to /ə/ and /ɪ/. Three common ways to show which syllables have non-reduced vowels (that is, a medium level of stress) are a *low* accent mark, as in (f), or a *high* accent mark that is *lighter and thinner* than the high accent mark for primary stress, as in (g), or that *slants to the left*, as in (h).

In addition, to show how many syllables a word has, dictionaries often put dashes (-) or dots (·) between the syllables.

*The American Heritage Dictionary of the English Language, Dell, 1980.
‡The Longman Dictionary of American English, Longman, 1983.
‡Webster's Ninth New Collegiate Dictionary, Merriam-Webster, 1987.
§The New Horizon Ladder Dictionary of the English Language, Signet, 1970.

Note: You will need to have a dictionary with pronunciation symbols to do the activities in this chapter.

Exercise 1: Dictionary Activity

Look up the following words in your dictionary. How many syllables does the word have? Write the number of syllables in the parentheses after each word. Which syllable has the strongest stress? Underline it.

1. educational (4)

2. airport ( )

3. karate ( )

4. language ( )

5. unusual ( )

6. curious ( )

7. marriage ( )

8. photographer ( )

9. especially ( )

10. aerobic ( )

Part II: Consonant and Vowel Sounds in the Dictionary

There are 26 letters in the English alphabet but approximately 39 sounds! As you know, some sounds, especially vowels, have many different spellings. There aren't enough letters to represent all of the sounds, so different sets of symbols have been developed to show their pronunciation.

The symbols used in *Sound Advantage* are in the first column, and symbols for other commonly used dictionaries follow.

Consonants: Commonly Used Symbols

Key Word	Sound Advantage	Longman Dictionary of American English	Webster's Ninth New Collegiate Dictionary	Longman Dictionary of Contemporary English	Horizon Ladder Dictionary of the English Language	Your Dictionary
1. put	p	p	p	p	p	
2. bus	b	b	b	b	b	
3. ten	t	t	t	t	t	
4. do	d	d	d	d	d	
5. cat	k	k	k	k	k	
6. game	g	g	g	g	g	
7. fun	f	f	f	f	f	
8. very	v	v	v	v	v	
9. think	θ	θ	th	θ	θ	
10. them	ð	ð	th	ð	ð	
11. say	s	s	s	s	s	
12. zoo	z	z	z	z	z	
13. ship	ʃ	ʃ	sh	ʃ	š	
14. measure	ʒ	ʒ	zh	ʒ	ž	
15. choose	tʃ	tʃ	ch	tʃ	č	
16. jet	dʒ	dʒ	j	dʒ	ǰ	
17. room	r	r	r	r	r	
18. luck	l	l	l	l	l	
19. move	m	m	m	m	m	
20. not	n	n	n	n	n	
21. sing	ŋ	ŋ	ŋ	ŋ	ŋ	
22. yes	y	y	y	y	y	
23. want	w	w	w	w	w	
24. hope	h	h	h	h	h	

Vowels: Commonly Used Symbols

Key Word	Sound Advantage	Longman Dictionary of American English	Webster's Ninth New Collegiate Dictionary	Longman Dictionary of Contemporary English	Horizon Ladder Dictionary of the English Language	Your Dictionary
1. keep	iy	i^y	ē	i:/i	iy	
2. sit	I	I	i	I	i	
3. take	ey	e^y	ā	eI	ey	
4. get	ɛ	ɛ	e	e	e	
5. bad	æ	æ	a	æ	æ	
6. bird	ər	3r	ər	3:/3	ər	
7. cut	ə	ʌ/ə	ə	ʌ/ə	ə	
8. stop	a	ɑ	ä	ɑ:/ɑ	a	
9. move	uw	u^w	ü	u:	uw	
10. good	ʊ	ʊ	u̇	ʊ	u	
11. go	ow	o^w	ō	əʊ	ow	
12. born	ɔ	ɔ	ȯ	ɔ:/ɔ	ɔ	
13. night	ay	aI	ī	aI	ay	
14. town	aw	aʊ	au̇	aʊ	aw	
15. boy	oy	ɔI	ȯi	ɔI	oy	

Exercise 2: Dictionary Activity

Part A: Look up each key word in your dictionary and write down the symbol that **your** dictionary uses for the underlined sound. (Only write the symbol for the **underlined part**, not the whole word.)

Part B: Practice pronouncing the key words. Pay special attention to the sound of the underlined part of the word. (Optional)

Exercise 3: Dictionary Activity

Below are some common English words. The common American pronunciations are written according to the symbols of *Sound Advantage*. Decide what words the symbols represent by pronouncing them to yourself and write them. Then, look up the word in **your** dictionary and copy the pronunciation symbols that it uses.

Pronunciation symbols used in this book	Normal spelling of the word	Pronunciation symbols used in your dictionary
1. /yɛs-tər-dey/	yesterday	
2. /kwes-tʃən/		
3. /məs-teyk/		
4. /θər-stiy/		
5. /wʊ-mən/		
6. /kæ-mər-ə/		
7. /gʊd-bay/		
8. /fyuw/		

Exercise 4: Dictionary Activity

Look up the pronunciation of the following words in your dictionary. Write their phonetic spelling (pronunciation symbols). Then practice pronouncing these words with a partner. Remember to pay attention to the stress. Check to see if your dictionary agrees with your partner's.

Pronunciation symbols from your dictionary

1. rhythm
2. salmon
3. pretzel
4. giraffe
5. anxiety
6. ridiculous
7. iron
8. torture
9. tissue
10. theme
11. refrigerator

12. towel

13. enthusiastic

14. hamburger

15. allergic

Exercise 5: Optional Homework

1. Write down eight words that you want to learn to pronounce. They could be words that you have tried to say but people could not understand or words from your reading.
2. Find each of your eight words in the dictionary and copy the phonetic spelling.
3. Copy an example sentence which uses each of your words. The sentence can come from your dictionary, your reading, or you can write it yourself.
4. Practice pronouncing your words and example sentences.
5. Dictate (read aloud) your eight words to a native speaker, whose job it is to write them down. Read the word, then the word in its sentence (to make its meaning clearer), and then read the word again.
6. After you have finished dictating all eight words, see if the native speaker wrote them down correctly. Discuss any misunderstandings.
7. Finally, ask the native speaker to pronounce the words for you.

1

Syllable Recognition and Reduction

PRETEST

Listen to the following words. Write the number of syllables next to the word.

1. _____ bad
2. _____ friendly
3. _____ radio
4. _____ perfect
5. _____ everything

6. _____ English
7. _____ doctor
8. _____ beautiful
9. _____ mail
10. _____ death

Part I: Syllables

	syllables	Every word in English has one or more syllables. A syllable always has a vowel sound and usually contains a consonant sound between it and the next syllable. One problem for students when pronouncing English is making too many or too few syllables.
(a) doctor	(2)	
(b) every	(2)	
(c) radio	(3)	
(d) thing	(1)	When you count syllables, try to listen for the "break" in the word that separates the syllables.
(e) probably (2 or 3)		Native speakers sometimes disagree about how many syllables a word has, as in (e). Listen to your teacher or people where you live to find out what is usual for your area.

Exercise 1: Listening

Listen to the following words. Write the number of syllables next to each word.

1. _____ listen   6. _____ general
2. _____ marriage   7. _____ lazy
3. _____ delicious   8. _____ memory
4. _____ vegetables   9. _____ breathe
5. _____ business   10. _____ ability

Part II: Stressed Syllables

(a) agreé ment (b) todáy (c) engineér	In English, words of more than one syllable have both stressed (strong) and unstressed (weak) syllables. In many languages, all the syllables are equal. But in English, there is both strong and weak stress.
(d) aeró bic (e) Árabic	Stress helps the listener to understand the word, and without correct stress, words can be misunderstood, as in (d) and (e). That is why it is very important to learn correct word stress.

Exercise 2: Listening

Listen to the following words. Write an accent mark over the syllable that is stressed (stronger) in each word.

1. cómfort   6. pronunciation
2. ability   7. disagree
3. arrangement   8. openness
4. unusual   9. architecture
5. excite   10. mountaineering

If you had trouble recognizing the stressed syllable, the following sections will give you more help.

Part III: Recognizing Syllable Stress in English

(a) ba n̂a na	When listening for the stressed syllable in a word, there are three things that can help you: 1. The **pitch is higher** in the stressed syllable than in the syllable before it.
(b) bȧ n̄a ṅa	2. The **vowel is longer** in the stressed syllable.
(c) bə næ nə	3. The vowel in the stressed syllable is pronounced as a **full vowel**; that is, it is not reduced to /ə/ or /I/, or dropped.*

*See Part C of this section for an explanation of /ə/ and Part IV for the dropping of some sounds in English.

Part A: Pitch Patterns

(a) tîme (b) knôw	There are different pitch patterns. When the stressed word is just ONE syllable, its pitch rises and falls in that ONE syllable. This is called **glide-down** pitch.
(c) alîve (d) recôrd	This also occurs in a word with more than one syllable when the stressed syllable comes at the end of the word, as in (c) and (d).
(e) tomôrrow (f) educâtional	When the stressed syllable is NOT the final syllable in a word or sentence, you will hear the pitch go up at the beginning of the syllable and **stay up** until the next syllable starts, as in (e) and (f). Then the pitch **steps down**.
	It is more important at this point that you can recognize where the pitch goes up, rather than identify exactly which pattern is occurring.

Exercise 3: Listening

Put an accent mark (ˆ) over the part of the word that has the higher pitch.

1. time	5. late
2. alive	6. record
3. engineer	7. fun
4. occur	8. temperature

Again, note that when the stressed word is just one syllable, its pitch rises (goes up) and falls (glides down) in that ONE syllable.

Exercise 4: Production

Practice the glide-down pattern by counting from one to ten. (Note that "seven" is step-down.)

1. one	6. six
2. two	7. seven
3. three	8. eight
4. four	9. nine
5. five	10. ten

Exercise 5: Listening and Production

Listen to the following sentences. Focus on the boldface words. Then practice saying these words and pay special attention to the glide-down pitch in the last syllable.

1. I don't have **time**.	time
2. Who **knows**?	knows
3. The class is **full**.	full
4. It's **alive**.	alive
5. Come at eight o'clock **tonight**.	tonight
6. Why are they **depressed**?	depressed

Exercise 6: Listening and Production (Optional)

Same as before.

1. What's he going to **record**?	record
2. That was a **command**.	command
3. I want to be **surprised**.	surprised
4. She's an **engineer**.	engineer
5. Don't **interfere**.	interfere
6. You must have **misunderstood**.	misunderstood

Exercise 7: Listening and Production

Listen to the following sentences. Then practice saying the boldface words with the step-down pattern.

1. When is the end of the **semester**?	semester
2. I bought a new **record**.	record
3. They need to study **grammar**.	grammar
4. We talked to him **yesterday**.	yesterday
5. What did you do on your **birthday**?	birthday
6. Who's your **teacher**?	teacher

Exercise 8: Listening and Production (Optional)

Same as before.

1. Turn off the **television**.	television
2. He said he was **unhappy**.	unhappy
3. Let's **celebrate**!	celebrate
4. She dressed **expensively**.	expensively
5. You **promised** us.	promised
6. What great **weather** we've been having!	weather
7. Listen for the stressed **syllable**.	syllable
8. Who's **responsibility** is it?	responsibility

Part B: Vowel Length

(a) āctȯr

(b) •ēxpress⎯

(c) ⎯permȧnėnt

(d) ⎯paymėnt

> The second very important feature of stressed syllables is that they are usually much longer than unstressed syllables.

Exercise 9: Listening and Production

Part A: Listen to the following words. Listen for the longest syllable in each word. Draw a line (—) over the longest syllable.

1. ōpen
2. lighter
3. support
4. enable
5. attractive
6. contain
7. undo
8. hospital
9. politeness
10. fatigue

Part B: With a partner, practice pronouncing the words in this exercise. Concentrate on making the marked syllables very long.

Exercise 10: Listening and Production

Listen to the following words, first pronounced in a sentence and then alone. Mark the longest syllable in each boldface word. Then practice pronouncing these words.

1. What are you **doing**?   doing

2. **Nothing** is the **matter**.   nothing

                                                          matter

3. What kind of **medicine** are you **using**?   medicine

                                                          using

4. Those **flowers** are **beautiful**.   flowers

                                                          beautiful

5. They want a **divorce** as soon as **possible**.	divorce
	possible
6. He **relaxed** for a few **minutes**.	relaxed
	minutes
7. Get **control** of **yourself**.	control
	yourself
8. She **escaped** the **danger**.	escaped
	danger

Part C: Reduced Syllables — The Schwa /ə/

a. *believe*	bəlieve	As you read before, if a word has more than one syllable, one syllable is strong and the other(s) weak. The vowel in the weak syllable is usually reduced to "uh." In dictionaries and pronunciation books, you will see this symbol: /ə/. It is called a *schwa*, and the pronunciation is "uh."* This is the vowel that English speakers produce most naturally and easily when their mouths are relaxed.†
b. *divorce*	dəvorce	
c. *advice*	ədvice	
d. *responsible*	rəsponsəbəl	
e. *development*	dəveləpmənt	
f. *going*	goən	Note that *-ing* and *-ion* endings, as in (f)–(i) are pronounced with /ə/.
g. hav*ing*	havən	
h. quest*ion*	questən	
i. comprehens*ion*	comprehensən	
		The schwa is the most important vowel sound in English because it occurs more often than any other vowel. Pronouncing most unstressed vowels as a schwa is very important for the rhythm of English. Also, by listening for /ə/, you can learn to better recognize the STRESSED syllable.

*In some dialects, /I/ is used instead of /ə/ (e.g., divorce = /dI/).
†People learning to speak English often make the mistake of pronouncing unstressed vowels the way they are spelled. But you will be more easily understood if you pronounce unstressed syllables with a short "uh" sound.

Exercise 11: Listening

Part A: Listen for /ə/ in the following words.

1. believe
2. having
3. listen
4. often

5. control
6. atomic
7. visit
8. police

9. receive
10. politics

Part B: Mark the reduced syllable with /ə/.

Example: bĕlieve

SCHWA ARTICULATION

To form /ə/:

Tongue position: low   (middle)   high

front   (center)   back

Tense vs. lax: relaxed

Tip: Say /iy/ as in "meet." Bring your tongue back and down a little. This will help you form /ə/.

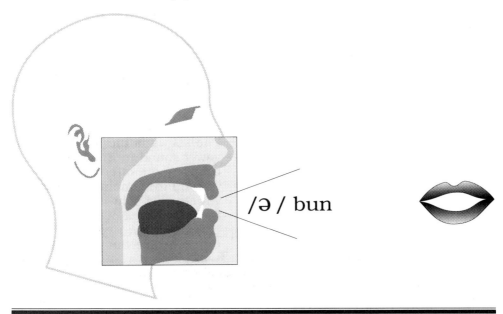

/ə / bun

Exercise 12: Listening and Production

Part A: Write /ə/ over the reduced vowels in each word.

1. təmorrow
2. hello
3. erase
4. depressed
5. marriage
6. driving

7. reply
8. mistake
9. delicious
10. chemical
11. second
12. receipt

Part B: Find a partner. Practice pronouncing the words in this exercise. Your teacher will listen as you practice.

Exercise 13: Listening and Production

Same as before.

1. dəvorce
2. going
3. animal
4. escape
5. logical

6. behave
7. direction
8. wanted
9. information
10. between

Part IV: Ellipsis

(a) favorite	fav'rite
(b) probably	pro'bly
(c) general	gen'ral
(d) business	bus'ness

In many dialects, unstressed syllables are not reduced to /ə/. Instead, they are completely dropped. This is called **ellipsis**.

Please note that although ellipsis is quite common, it is not used by all speakers.

Exercise 14: Listening and Production

Part A: Listen to the following words. Cross out the dropped syllable in each.

1. memøry	5. vegetables	9. conference
2. mineral	6. separate	10. interesting
3. margarine	7. average	11. probably
4. Florida	8. suppose	12. favorite

Part B: Find a partner. Practice pronouncing the words in this exercise. Your teacher will listen as you practice.

Exercise 15: Production

Cross out the dropped syllable. Practicing pronouncing each word with ellipsis.

1. famįly	6. finally	11. federal
2. business	7. every	12. operator
3. horrible	8. evening	13. practically
4. camera	9. generally	14. difference
5. memory	10. aspirin	15. opera

Exercise 16: Production

Sometimes in very casual speech, the beginning of the word is dropped. This is another kind of ellipsis.

You can also use an /ə/ for these words. Practice pronouncing both patterns for the following words.

1. especially	əspecially	'specially
2. another	ənother	'nother
3. because	bəcause	'cause
4. remember	rəmember	'member
5. about	əbout	'bout
6. enough	ənough	'nough

Exercise 17: Production

Practice pronouncing the following phrases with the first sound dropped and then with /ə/.

1. 'bout eight	əbout eight
2. 'nough time	ənough time
3. 'member that	rəmember that
4. 'specially nice	əspecially nice
5. 'nother one	ənother one
6. 'cause she said so	bəcause she said so

Exercise 18: Production

Practice pronouncing the following phrases. Focus on /ə/ and ellipsis.

1. horrible memory	6. evening conference
2. difficult visit	7. average marriage
3. delicious vegetables	8. finally comfortable
4. family business	9. mistaken reply
5. telephone operator	10. probably divorce

Part V: Unstressed Syllables with Non-Reduced Vowels

(a) main**tain**

(b) **pass**port

(c) ho**tel**

(d) **ta**xicab

You have learned that words generally have syllables that are stressed and unstressed and that the **unstressed** syllables are pronounced with the reduced vowel /ə/, as in the words "because" and "common."

However, occasionally there are words that have unstressed syllables, but the vowels are **not reduced**, as in (a) through (d).

Even though the syllable is unstressed, it will sound **longer** than a reduced syllable. (This is often called secondary, or medium stress.)

Exercise 19: Listening and Production

Part A: When listening to the following words, compare the italicized syllable in column A with the italicized syllable in column B. (Don't worry about the meaning of the words; they have been chosen only to show you the contrast in stress.)

A (reduced to /ə/)	B (not reduced)
1. *com*pose	inter*com*
2. *ba*tik	acro*bat*
3. cele*bra*tory	cele*brate*
4. *ca*noe	soup *can*
5. in*to*nation	toma*to*
6. *be*lligerent	door*bell*
7. plen*ti*ful	plen*ty*
8. in*su*lation	in*sult*

Part B: Pronounce the words in column A. Pronounce the words in column B. Then pronounce 1 (A and B); 2 (A and B), etc.

Exercise 20: Listening and Production

Part A: Listen to the following words. Decide if the italicized un-stressed syllable is reduced or not. If it is reduced, write /ə/ over it.

1. prom*ise*	5. *Ja*pan	9. class*es*
2. a*tom*	6. for*eign*	10. acc*ess*
3. mail*box*	7. base*ball*	
4. air*port*	8. lim*it*	

Part B: Check your answers. Then practice pronouncing these words with a partner. Be careful to show the difference between the longer syllables, where the vowels are not reduced, and the shorter syllables, where the vowels are reduced to /ə/.

Exercise 21: Listening and Production (Optional)

Same as before.

1. *united*	4. tooth*paste*	7. kitch*en*
2. Chi*na*	5. *develop*	8. *apart*ment
3. in*dex*	6. *ex*change	

Exercise 22: Interview

Part A: Interview two native* speakers of English. Write their answers in the blanks, and remember to have them sign their names. When asking your questions, focus especially on reduced syllables and ellipsis. Study each question before you speak so that you do not have to read it. You may want to practice with a partner first.

1. What is your favorite memory?
2. Where are you the most comfortable?
3. Have you ever tried aerobic exercise?
4. What is impossible for you to believe?
5. What will you probably do this evening?
6. What is a difficult job for you?
7. Which is healthier: butter or margarine?
8. What do you not do naturally?
9. What is your general idea about marriage?
10. Who do you never believe?

Answers:

1.	1.
2.	2.
3.	3.
4.	4.
5.	5.
6.	6.
7.	7.
8.	8.
9.	9.
10.	10.

_____ (signature)   _____ (signature)

*Many exercises in this text call for the participation of native speakers. However, if students are in their own countries, this may not be possible. In such cases, practice with classmates is recommended or, on occasion, practice with other English instructors.

Part B: Report your answers to the class or small group your teacher assigns.

Exercise 23: Dictation

Choose ten words from this chapter and write them below. Dictate them to a native speaker or another student in the class. Compare answers when you are finished.

1.   6.

2.   7.

3.   8.

4.   9.

5.   10.

An Overview of English Vowels

English vowel sounds cause problems for nonnative speakers for several reasons.

First, compared with many languages, English has a large number of vowels — 15 in all. Another reason is that many languages have only one lax vowel, /a/, whereas English has seven.

In addition, many languages have pure vowels, but many of the vowels in English are not pure. This means they are lengthened and spoken with the tongue moving from one sound into another sound (into the semi-vowels /y/ or /w/).

The diphthongs (double vowels) /ay/, /aw/, and /oy/, have the most tongue movement, but the tense vowels (/iy/, /ey/, /uw/, /ow/) are also written with two letters because they also have some diphthong-like tongue and face movement.

Following are the 12 main vowel sounds in English and the three diphthongs. They are organized and described in terms of four characteristics:

a. how HIGH or LOW the tongue position is in the mouth;
b. how far FRONT or BACK the tongue is;
c. how TENSE or LAX (relaxed) the muscles of the tongue, mouth, and face are;
d. whether the lips are ROUNDED or UNROUNDED.

		Front	Center	Back
High	Tense	iy (beat)	ər (bird)	uw (boot)
	Lax	I (bit)		ʊ (book)
Middle	Tense	ey (bait)		ow (boat)
	Lax	ɛ (bet)	ə (but)	
Low	Tense			
	Lax	æ (bat)	a (body)	ɔ (bored)
		Unrounded	Unrounded	Rounded

Diphthongs:

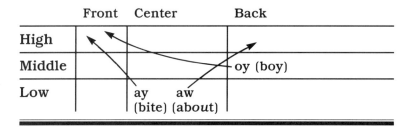

	Front	Center	Back
High			
Middle			oy (boy)
Low		ay aw	
		(bite) (about)	

The following vowel symbols are used in this text:

/iy/	beat
/I/	bit
/ey/	bait
/ɛ/	bet
/æ/	bad
/ər/	bird
/ə/	bun
/a/	body
/uw/	boot
/ʊ/	book
/ow/	boat
/ɔ/	bored
/ay/	buy
/aw/	about
/oy/	boy

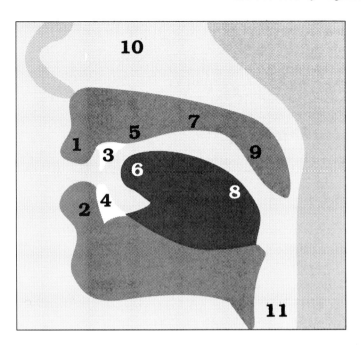

1. Upper lip
2. Lower lip
3. Upper front teeth
4. Lower front teeth
5. Tooth ridge
6. Tongue tip
7. Hard palate
8. Back of tongue
9. Soft palate
10. Nasal cavity
11. Airway

2

Lax Vowels

PRETEST A

Put a check next to the words that have the /ae/ sound, as in "mad."

1. _____ answer

2. _____ fashion

3. _____ caller

4. _____ army

5. _____ hall

6. _____ past

7. _____ slang

8. _____ has

9. _____ as

10. _____ farther

Part I: /ae/

a. **half**
b. **math**
c. **athlete**
d. **answer**

This is a very relaxed vowel. Your mouth must open. The sides go out and down a bit.

The spelling for this sound is **a**.

Exercise 1: Listening

You will hear a pair of words. Circle if they are the same or different.

1. same   different

2. same   different

3. same   different

4. same   different

5. same   different

Check your answers.

6. same   different

7. same   different

8. same   different

9. same   different

10. same   different

Exercise 2: Listening

You will hear three words. Two words will have the /ae/ sound and one will be different. Put an X on the blank for the word that is different.

	1	2	3
1.	_____	_____	_____
2.	_____	_____	_____
3.	_____	_____	_____
4.	_____	_____	_____
5.	_____	_____	_____

Check your answers.

6. _____   _____   _____

7. _____   _____   _____

8. _____   _____   _____

9. _____   _____   _____

10. _____   _____   _____

Exercise 3: Listening

Look at the following word groups. Two words in each group will have the vowel sound /ae/ in the first syllable and one will be different. Put a check next to the word that has a different vowel sound.

1. _____ apple   _____ apply   _____ answer

2. _____ bath   _____ water   _____ pattern

3. _____ material   _____ mass   _____ match

4. _____ add   _____ addition   _____ ad

5. _____ fashion   _____ blast   _____ bald

Now you will hear these words. Check your answers.

Hint: To practice relaxed vowels, take a rubber band and stretch it out as you say the vowel. This will help you "see" the length of the vowel.

ARTICULATION

To form /ae/:

Tongue position: (low)   middle   high

(front)   center   back

Face, jaw, and tongue: relaxed

Mouth position: wide

Sound focus: (Close your eyes.) Open your mouth. Feel your lips spread back. Rest your tongue at the bottom of your mouth. It should be relaxed and wide (spread out). The tip can touch the lower teeth. This is the position you want. (Try not to drop your jaw when you make the sound.)

Tip: Say the word "as" and smile.

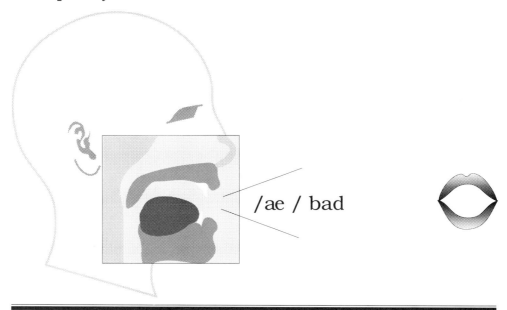

/ae / bad

Exercise 4: Production

Practice pronouncing the following words.

1. laugh	6. Jan	11. dance
2. math	7. lamb	12. Japan
3. Saturday	8. as	13. fat
4. answer	9. grammar	14. plant
5. matter	10. had	15. balance

Exercise 5: Production

Same as before.

1. bath	6. attack	11. snack
2. pattern	7. family	12. last
3. advertisement	8. animal	13. afternoon
4. past	9. happy	14. practical
5. dad	10. slang	15. examination

Exercise 6: Production

Practice pronouncing the following sentences.

1. I have math class now.
2. Dad's studying the family's past.
3. I heard the ad Saturday afternoon.
4. That answer made Jan mad.

PRETEST B

Put a check next to the words that have the /I/ sound, as in "big."

1. _____ his
2. _____ feel
3. _____ mystery
4. _____ winter
5. _____ pretty

6. _____ this
7. _____ her
8. _____ women
9. _____ enter
10. _____ live (verb)

Part II: /I/

(a) th**i**s	This vowel can be very difficult because it is very relaxed. It is easy to confuse with the vowel /i/, as in the word "meet."
(b) w**i**nner	Notice that sometimes the spelling "i" does not represent the sound, as in (c) and (d).
(c) w**o**men	
(d) b**u**siness	Other spellings: y: mystery e: pretty

Exercise 7: Listening

You will hear a pair of words. Circle if they are the same or different.

1. same   different
2. same   different
3. same   different

4. same   different

5. same   different

Check your answers.

6. same   different

7. same   different

8. same   different

9. same   different

10. same   different

Exercise 8: Listening

You will hear three words. Two words will have the /I/ sound and one will be different. Put an X on the blank for the word that is different.

	1	2	3
1.	_____	_____	_____
2.	_____	_____	_____
3.	_____	_____	_____
4.	_____	_____	_____
5.	_____	_____	_____

Check your answers.

6.	_____	_____	_____
7.	_____	_____	_____
8.	_____	_____	_____
9.	_____	_____	_____
10.	_____	_____	_____

Exercise 9: Listening

Look at the following word groups. Two words in each group will have the vowel sound (I) and one will be different. Put a check next to the word that has a different vowel sound.

1. _____	fin	_____	feet	_____	fit
2. _____	knit	_____	neat	_____	nip
3. _____	itch	_____	each	_____	it
4. _____	will	_____	wish	_____	well

Now you will hear these words. Check your answers.

5. _____	busy	_____	dizzy	_____	diaper
6. _____	these	_____	this	_____	think
7. _____	issue	_____	insure	_____	item
8. _____	did	_____	dead	_____	dill

Now you will hear these words. Check your answers.

ARTICULATION

To form /I/:

Tongue position: low   middle   ⟨high⟩
                        ⟨front⟩   center   back

Face, jaw, and tongue: relaxed

Mouth position: wide

Sound focus: (Close your eyes.) Say /i/ as in "meet." Feel that your tongue is very tight. Now relax it. Also relax your face and jaw. This is the position you want.

Tip: Most languages have the /i/ sound, as in "meet." For the /I/ sound, your tongue is in the same position except that it is VERY relaxed. Say /i/ and then RELAX your tongue without moving it. This is the /I/ sound.

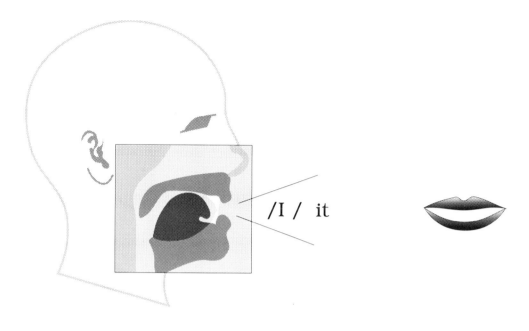

/I / it

Exercise 10: Production

Practice pronouncing the following words.

1. give	6. single	11. film
2. live	7. busy	12. mix
3. pretty	8. sick	13. quickly
4. interest	9. if	14. skill
5. quiz	10. Mr.	15. middle

Exercise 11: Production

Same as before.

1. it	6. think
2. different	7. gym
3. Mrs.	8. fiction
4. in	9. ill
5. kiss	10. his

Exercise 12: Production

Practice pronouncing the following sentences.

1. His sister's sick.
2. It's pretty interesting.
3. I think Mr. Smith's in the gym.
4. Mix in some dill.

PRETEST C

Put a check next to the words that have the /ε/ sound, as in "bed."

1. _____ medium   6. _____ extra

2. _____ measure   7. _____ entrance

3. _____ letter   8. _____ Wednesday

4. _____ read (past tense)   9. _____ again

5. _____ heard   10. _____ wear

Part III: /ε/

(a) **empty**	/ε/ is often confused with /ey/, as in "ate," and /ae/, as in "had."
(b) **head**	The spelling is usually "e" but note the other spellings:
(c) ag**ai**n	ea: dead
(d) **any**	ai: said
	a: Mary

Exercise 13: Listening

You will hear a pair of words. Circle if they are the same or different.

1. same   different

2. same   different

3. same   different

4. same   different

5. same   different

Check your answers.

  6. same   different

  7. same   different

  8. same   different

  9. same   different

10. same   different

Exercise 14: Listening

You will hear three words. Two words will have the /ɛ/ sound and one will be different. Put an X on the blank for the word that is different.

	1	2	3
1.	___	___	___
2.	___	___	___
3.	___	___	___
4.	___	___	___
5.	___	___	___

Check your answers.

	1	2	3
6.	___	___	___
7.	___	___	___
8.	___	___	___
9.	___	___	___
10.	___	___	___

Exercise 15: Listening

Look at the following word groups. Two words in each group will have the vowel sound /ɛ/ and one will be different. Put a check next to the word that has a different vowel sound.

1. ___ bead   ___ bed   ___ deaf

2. ___ wed   ___ weed   ___ well

3. _____ says   _____ say   _____ September

4. _____ debt   _____ below   _____ effort

5. _____ paint   _____ bend   _____ rent

6. _____ head   _____ hate   _____ hell

Now you will hear these words. Check your answers.

ARTICULATION

To form /ɛ/:

Tongue position: low   (middle)   high

(front)   center   back

Face, jaw, and tongue: relaxed

Mouth position: wide

Sound focus: (Close your eyes.) Say /ey/ as in late. Feel that your tongue is very tight. Now relax it. Also relax your face and jaw. This is the position you want. Do not smile as you do for the /ey/ sound.

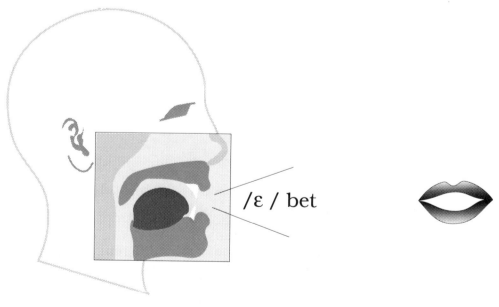

/ɛ / bet

Exercise 16: Production

Practice pronouncing the following words.

1. says	6. enter
2. when	7. measure
3. death	8. Wednesday
4. sense	9. wear
5. gel	10. marry

Exercise 17: Production

Same as before.

1. section	6. Mexico
2. leather	7. weather
3. breakfast	8. heaven
4. pear	9. seven
5. heavy	10. extra

Exercise 18: Production

Practice pronouncing the following sentences.

1. I need seven extra.
2. When did they get married?
3. Let's order eggs for breakfast.
4. The gel's on the shelf.

PRETEST D

Put a check next to the words that have the /a/ sound, as in "water."

1. _____ bottle	6. _____ money	11. _____ Don
2. _____ calm	7. _____ son	12. _____ cough
3. _____ hold	8. _____ shock	13. _____ palm
4. _____ box	9. _____ shot	14. _____ talk
5. _____ lot	10. _____ front	15. _____ hard

Part IV: /a/

a. d**o**ctor	Although it is often spelled with the letter "o," this vowel is NOT pronounced with the /o/ sound. Rather, the sound is "ah," as in the word "want."
b. cl**o**th	Other spellings:
c. d**o**llar	a: watch ou: bought au: author* aw: lawn*

*In some dialects, these words are pronounced as /ɔ/. See Teacher's Manual for an explanation of this sound.

Exercise 19: Listening

You will hear a pair of words. Circle if they are the same or different.

1. same   different

2. same   different

3. same   different

4. same   different

5. same   different

Check your answers.

6. same   different

7. same   different

8. same   different

9. same   different

10. same   different

Exercise 20: Listening

You will hear three words. Two words will have the /a/ sound and one will be different. Put an X on the blank for the word that is different.

	1	2	3
1.	_____	_____	_____
2.	_____	_____	_____
3.	_____	_____	_____
4.	_____	_____	_____
5.	_____	_____	_____

Check your answers.

	1	2	3
6.	_____	_____	_____
7.	_____	_____	_____
8.	_____	_____	_____
9.	_____	_____	_____
10.	_____	_____	_____

Exercise 21: Listening

Look at the following word groups. Two words in each group will have the vowel sound /a/ and one will be different. Put a check next to the word that has a different vowel sound.

1. _____ cloth   _____ common   _____ country
2. _____ glove   _____ body   _____ Tom
3. _____ pocket   _____ packet   _____ rocket
4. _____ possible   _____ collar   _____ passible

Now you will hear these words. Check your answers.

5. _____ sought   _____ shot   _____ rough
6. _____ other   _____ mosque   _____ gone
7. _____ Polish   _____ promise   _____ polish
8. _____ popular   _____ Monday   _____ daughter

Now you will hear these words. Check your answers.

ARTICULATION

To form /a/:

Tongue position: (low)   middle   high

front   (center)   back

Face, jaw, and tongue: relaxed

Mouth position: wide

Sound focus: (Close your eyes.) Open your mouth wide. Relax your tongue. Feel it resting on the bottom of your mouth. Drop your lower jaw a little. This is the position you want.

Tip: Imagine you are at the doctor's. Open your mouth and say "ahhh."

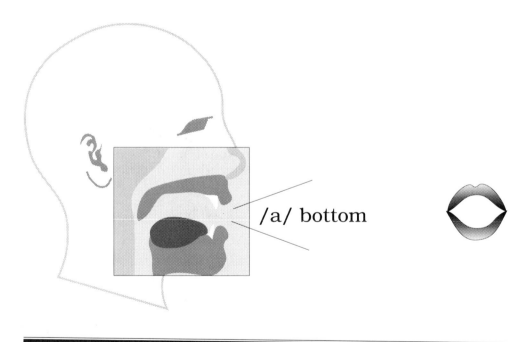

/a/ bottom

Exercise 22: Production

Practice pronouncing the following words.

1. stop
2. block
3. problem
4. lock
5. Bob

6. odd
7. possible
8. bald*
9. lawn*
10. brought*

11. probably
12. operate
13. gone*
14. blonde
15. author*

Exercise 23: Production

Same as before.

1. mosque
2. bought*
3. doctor
4. topic
5. call*

6. coffee*
7. college
8. popular
9. process
10. body

11. honest
12. copy
13. hospital
14. yawn*
15. model

Exercise 24: Production

Practice pronouncing the following sentences.

1. I bought a lot.
2. The doctor's not at the hospital.
3. It's a popular college.
4. Honestly, it's a problem.

Exercise 25: Spelling† (Optional)

Part A. You have probably noticed that the most common spelling for the sound /a/ is: **o** + consonant(s). Listen and fill in the banks for the missing sounds.

1. r__ck
2. p__t
3. c__llege
4. m__nster

5. l__st*
6. sh__ck
7. d__ll*
8. sp__t

9. h__t d__g*
10. m__dern
11. h__spital
12. s__rry*

Find a partner. Practice pronouncing these words.

---

*In some dialects, these words are pronounced with /ɔ/.
†Unlike the other vowel sounds in this chapter, the spelling for this one has several difficult variations. If you have problems with the spelling of this sound, please complete this section.

Part B. Here is another way to spell the /a/ sound: **a** + consonants.

Note: /a/ + **l, r,** or **w** are very common spellings. Fill in the blanks for the missing sounds.

1. f__ther
2. b__ld*
3. t__ll*
4. f__r
5. w__ter*

6. h__rd
7. t__lk*
8. l__rge
9. l__w*
10. __wful*

11. p__rk
12. s__w*
13. b__rn
14. __lways*
15. l__wn*

Find a partner. Practice pronouncing these words.

Part C. au + consonant(s)
ou + consonant(s) } other common spellings.

Fill in the blanks for the missing sounds. Please note that all of the following can also be pronounced with /ɔ/.

1. l__ndry
2. t__ght
3. d__ghter
4. f__lt
5. b__ght
6. f__ght

7. c__ght
8. __tomatic
9. c__se
10. __ght
11. c__gh
12. __gust

Find a partner. Practice pronouncing these words.

Exercise 26: Review

Listen to the sound of the underlined letter(s) in each word. Put a check next to the words that have the /a/ sound in them.

1. _____ p<u>o</u>nd
2. _____ b<u>o</u>ttle
3. _____ <u>o</u>ver

4. _____ s<u>o</u>rry
5. _____ p<u>o</u>t
6. _____ t<u>a</u>lk

*In some dialects, these words are pronounced with /ɔ/.

7. _____ potato   9. _____ taught

8. _____ promise   10. _____ obvious

Exercise 27: Review

Fill in the blanks with the missing letters.

1. ___ff*   7. b___mb

2. c___ll*   8. p___pular

3. t___ght*   9. ___dd

4. f___nd   10. bl___nde

5. l___n*   11. D___n

6. c___mmon   12. l___ss

PRETEST E

Put a check next to the words that have the /ʊ/ sound, as in "book."

1. _____ should   6. _____ food

2. _____ blue   7. _____ full

3. _____ putting   8. _____ rule

4. _____ pool   9. _____ would

5. _____ cooked   10. _____ stood

Part V: /ʊ/

(a) t**oo**k	This sound is the only relaxed back vowel. Your lips are rounded, but not as tightly as for /uw/ (see Chapter 3, Part IV). Also, your tongue is high but not a high as for /uw/.
(b) f**oo**t	
(c) p**u**sh	
(d) p**u**ll	The spelling for this sound is often **oo**, **ou**, or **u**.
(e) w**ou**ld	

*In some dialects, these words are pronounced with /ɔ/.

Exercise 28: Listening

You will hear a pair of words. Circle if they are the same or different.

1. same   different

2. same   different

3. same   different

4. same   different

5. same   different

Check your answers.

6. same   different

7. same   different

8. same   different

9. same   different

10. same   different

Exercise 29: Listening

You will hear three words. Two words will have the /ʊ/ sound and one will be different. Put an X on the blank for the word that is different.

	1	2	3
1.	___	___	___
2.	___	___	___
3.	___	___	___
4.	___	___	___
5.	___	___	___

Check your answers.

6. _____ _____ _____

7. _____ _____ _____

8. _____ _____ _____

9. _____ _____ _____

10. _____ _____ _____

Exercise 30: Listening

Look at the following word groups. Two words in each group will have the vowel sound /ʊ/ in the first syllable and one will be different. Put a check next to the word that has a different vowel sound.

1. _____ cushion   _____ call   _____ couldn't

2. _____ shopping   _____ sure   _____ sugar

3. _____ doesn't   _____ butcher   _____ bullet

4. _____ woman   _____ woolen   _____ woven

5. _____ pudding   _____ goodness   _____ group

Now you will hear these words. Check your answers.

_____

ARTICULATION

To form /ʊ/:

Tongue position: low   middle   (high)

                  front   center   (back)

Face, jaw, and tongue: relaxed

Mouth position: lips a little rounded

                 teeth visible

Sound focus: (Close your eyes.) Say "uh" /ə/ and then round your lips just a little. Pull the back of your tongue up until its sides touch the edges of your back teeth. This is the position for /ʊ/.

Tip: Say the word "do" and then relax your tongue and lips a little. This will give you the /ʊ/ sound.

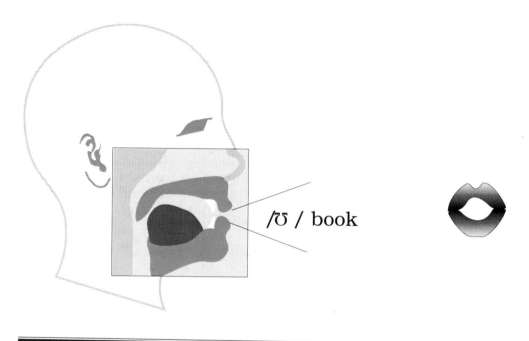

/ʊ / book

Exercise 31: Production

Practice pronouncing the following words.

1. could	6. good	11. would
2. pull	7. sugar	12. full
3. took	8. stood	13. put
4. should	9. look	14. books
5. wolf	10. woman	15. pushy

Exercise 32: Production

Same as before.

1. soot	6. bookshelf	11. understood
2. hook	7. woolen	12. butcher
3. childhood	8. pushed	13. cookie
4. input	9. cushion	14. rookie
5. wooden	10. bulletin	15. pussycat

Exercise 33: Production

Practice pronouncing the following phrases.

1. pushed and pulled
2. the pudding's good
3. a woolen hood
4. cookies full of sugar
5. the woman understood

6. a crooked bookshelf
7. we would cook
8. a wooden pulley
9. took a look
10. look for the hook in the brook

Exercise 34: Production

Practice pronouncing the following sentences.

1. You should look.
2. I want wooden bookshelves.
3. Did you cook chocolate pudding?
4. The woman works with a rookie.

Exercise 35: Production

Practice reading the following tongue twister.

How much wood would a woodchuck chuck if a woodchuck could chuck wood?

Exercise 36: Production

Practice reading the following riddles aloud. Be sure that you pronounce the boldface letters with the vowel /ʊ/.

1. If William's w**o**lf hound w**ou**ldn't walk in the w**oo**ds while William's washw**o**man w**ou**ld wash William's w**oo**len underwear,
how many w's are there in all?
Answer: None. There are no w's in "all."

2. What is f**u**ll of holes but can hold water?
Answer: A sponge.

For additional vowel practice, see Appendix C for work with contrasting vowels.

3

The Tense Vowels

PRETEST A

Put the following words into the correct column according to the diphthongs (double vowels) they contain.

pie	down	crowd
house	voice	join
now	sky	climb
coin	like	south
point	foil	choice
ice	night	hour

/ay/ (bite)	/aw/ (out)	/oy/ (boy)
_____	_____	_____
_____	_____	_____
_____	_____	_____
_____	_____	_____
_____	_____	_____
_____	_____	_____

Part I: Diphthongs /ay/, /aw/, /oy/

(a) sk**y**   /ay/

(b) l**ou**d   /aw/

(c) ch**oi**ce   /oy/

Many languages don't have diphthongs. English has three. They are double vowels with two equal parts that require a lot of mouth, tongue, and jaw movement. As a result, they are quite long.

Exercise 1: Listening

You will hear three words. Two words will have the same diphthong sound and one will be different. Put an X on the blank for the word that is different.

/ay/

	1	2	3
1.			
2.			
3.			
4.			
5.			

Check your answers.

/aw/

	1	2	3
6.			
7.			
8.			
9.			
10.			

Check your answers.

/oy/

| 11. | | | |
| 12. | | | |

13. _____   _____   _____

14. _____   _____   _____

15. _____   _____   _____

ARTICULATION

To form /ay/, /aw/, /oy/:

Face, jaw, tongue, and mouth position will change dramatically as you make these two-part sounds.

Sound Focus /ay/: (Close your eyes.) Lower your jaw. Relax and rest your tongue at the bottom of your mouth. Begin the sound /a/. Then move your jaw up until the lips are resting slightly open and spread. Move your tongue up and toward the front of your mouth to produce /y/.

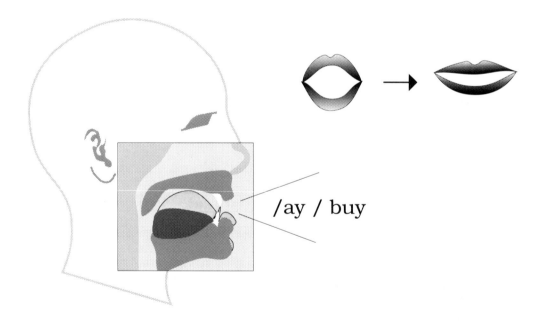

/ay / buy

Sound Focus /aw/: (Close your eyes.) Lower your jaw and move it a little forward. Rest your tongue at the bottom of your mouth. Begin the sound /a/ or /ae/. Then move your jaw up as you move your tongue up and back and round your lips to produce /w/.

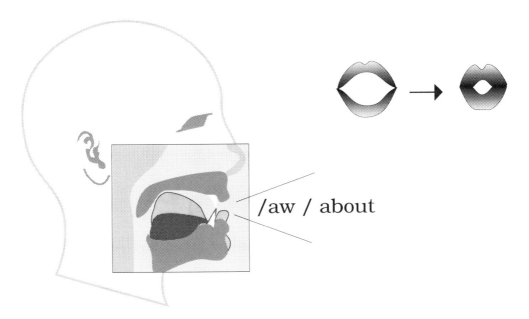

/aw / about

Sound Focus /oy/:   (Close your eyes.) Open and round your lips a little while pulling your tongue down and back in your mouth to begin the sound /o/. Then move your tongue high up and to the front and unround your lips to produce /y/.

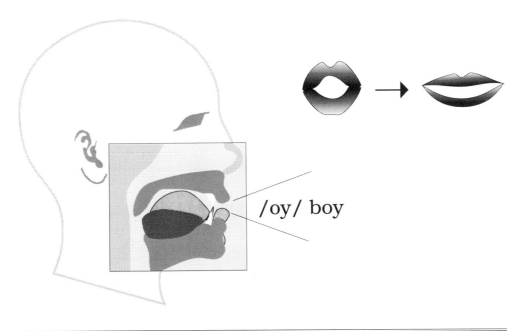

/oy/ boy

Exercise 2: Production /ay/

Practice pronouncing the following words.

1. eye	5. why're	9. diet
2. knife	6. pie	10. climb
3. typewriter	7. like	11. rise
4. quiet	8. bright	12. height

Exercise 3: Production /aw/

Same as before.

1. pound	5. south	9. thousand
2. loud	6. now	10. doubt
3. flower	7. crowd	11. flour
4. allow	8. amount	12. proud

Exercise 4: Production /oy/

Same as before.

1. choice	5. coin	9. avoid
2. point	6. enjoy	10. poison
3. oil	7. voice	11. boys
4. noise	8. annoyance	12. unemployment

Exercise 5: Production

Practice pronouncing the following sentences.

1. I'm annoyed by the noise.
2. The crowd became quiet.
3. The price of oil is climbing.
4. How will they avoid unemployment?
5. The noise is too loud. I can't hear your voice.
6. No doubt it's another high rise.

PRETEST B

Put a check next to the words that have the /iy/ sound, as in "me."

1. _____ these   5. _____ meter   9. _____ trees

2. _____ sleep   6. _____ is   10. _____ met

3. _____ sit   7. _____ live

4. _____ tried   8. _____ please

Part II: /iy/

(a) **ea**sy
(b) **lea**ving
(c) sh**e**
(d) n**ee**dy
(e) p**ie**ce

This is a very tense vowel. It is the highest front vowel. It has a pure /i/ sound followed by a /y/ glide, so it is very long and moves even closer to the top of your mouth at the end.

There are several spellings for this sound, including: **e**, **ee**, **ea**, **ie**.

Exercise 6: Listening

You will hear a pair of words. Circle if they are the same or different.

1. same   different

2. same   different

3. same   different

4. same   different

5. same   different

Check your answers.

6. same   different

7. same   different

8. same   different

9. same   different

10. same   different

Exercise 7: Listening

You will hear three words. Two words will have the /iy/ sound and one will be different. Put an X on the blank for the word that is different.

	1	2	3
1.	_____	_____	_____
2.	_____	_____	_____
3.	_____	_____	_____
4.	_____	_____	_____
5.	_____	_____	_____

Check your answers.

	1	2	3
6.	_____	_____	_____
7.	_____	_____	_____
8.	_____	_____	_____
9.	_____	_____	_____
10.	_____	_____	_____

Exercise 8: Listening

Look at the following word groups. Two words in each group will have the vowel sound /iy/ in the first syllable and one will be different. Put a check next to the word that has a different vowel sound.

1. _____ reached   _____ weight   _____ secret
2. _____ edge   _____ priest   _____ evening
3. _____ frequent   _____ people   _____ spread
4. _____ weren't   _____ meat   _____ fever
5. _____ equal   _____ neither   _____ rich

Now you will hear these words. Check your answers.

ARTICULATION

To form /iy/:

Tongue position: low   middle   (high)

front   center   back

Face, jaw, and tongue: tense

Mouth position: wide

Sound focus: (Close your eyes.) Open your mouth just a little and smile. Raise the front of your tongue as high as you can, leaving a very narrow space between the top of your tongue and the top of your mouth. Rest the tip of your tongue against the back of your lower front teeth. The sound begins with a pure /i/ and ends by the tongue moving even closer to the top of your mouth to form the /y/ part of the sound.

Tip: This is a long sound. It's called "tense" because the muscles of the tongue, lips, and corners of the mouth are all tight. You can feel the tension (tightness) under your chin, too.

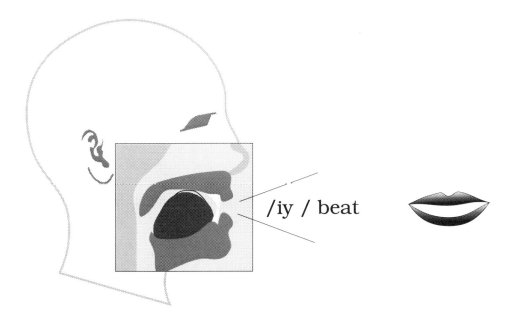

/iy / beat

Exercise 9: Production

Practice pronouncing the following words.

1. three	6. either	11. receive
2. eaten	7. feeling	12. wheels
3. mean	8. leisure	13. peace
4. key	9. teeth	14. pleased
5. people	10. reason	15. thief

Exercise 10: Production

Practice pronouncing the following phrases.

1. easy to read	8. breathe deeply
2. sweet dreams	9. secret meetings
3. please believe me	10. Ph.D. degree
4. weak tea	11. cheap gasoline
5. a CD	12. disease-free
6. chief of police	13. a piece of meat
7. cream cheese	14. street people

Exercise 11: Production

Practice pronouncing the following sentences.

1. She's feeling pleased.
2. It's the key to being free.
3. You mean he's the reason?
4. Meet me at three.

PRETEST C

Put a check next to the words that have the /ey/ sound, as in "they."

1.	_____ break	6.	_____ lead
2.	_____ leave	7.	_____ eight
3.	_____ happen	8.	_____ them
4.	_____ famous	9.	_____ place
5.	_____ radio	10.	_____ painful

Part III: /ey/

(a) **pay**d**ay**	This is a tense, long, mid-front vowel. It has a gliding movement of the tongue upward and forward, from pure /e/ to /y/, giving it a diphthong-like quality.
(b) r**ai**se	
(c) sh**a**pe	Some common spellings for this sound are **ai**, **ay**, and **eigh**.
(d) n**eigh**bor	

Exercise 12: Listening

You will hear a pair of words. Circle if they are the same or different.

    1. same   different

    2. same   different

    3. same   different

    4. same   different

    5. same   different

Check your answers.

    6. same   different

    7. same   different

    8. same   different

    9. same   different

   10. same   different

Exercise 13: Listening

You will hear three words. Two words will have the /ey/ sound and one will be different. Put an X on the blank for the word that is different.

         1   2   3

    1. _____   _____   _____

    2. _____   _____   _____

3. _____ _____ _____

4. _____ _____ _____

5. _____ _____ _____

Check your answers.

6. _____ _____ _____

7. _____ _____ _____

8. _____ _____ _____

9. _____ _____ _____

10. _____ _____ _____

Exercise 14: Listening

Look at the following word groups. Two words in each group will have the vowel sound /ey/ in the first syllable and one will be different. Put a check next to the word that has a different vowel sound.

1. _____ break   _____ change   _____ hand

2. _____ wheel   _____ paint   _____ favorite

3. _____ saw   _____ ache   _____ came

4. _____ said   _____ straighten _____ safety

5. _____ native   _____ ancient   _____ father

Now you will hear these words. Check your answers.

ARTICULATION

To form /ey/:

Tongue position: low   (middle)   high

front   center   back

Face, jaw, and tongue: tense

Mouth position: slightly smiling

Sound focus: (Close your eyes.) Push the middle of your tongue forward and up into the middle of your mouth. The tip of your tongue may touch behind the bottom front teeth. Open your lips and pull them back a little. As you make a pure /e/ sound, move your tongue up and more forward to finish with the sound /y/. (Your jaw will follow your tongue up.)

Tip: This is a very long sound. You should feel your tongue and jaw move up while you're pronouncing it. Feel the tenseness of it under your chin.

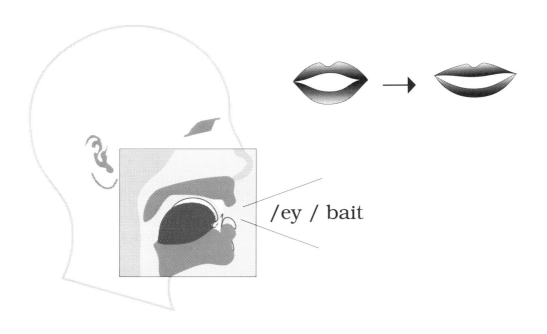

/ey / bait

Exercise 15: Production

Practice pronouncing the following words.

1. paper	6. vacation	11. stay
2. great	7. eight	12. straighten
3. plate	8. behavior	13. educate
4. radio	9. afraid	14. today
5. patient	10. pronunciation	15. female

Exercise 16: Production

Practice pronouncing the following phrases.

1. bake a cake
2. take a break
3. aches and pains
4. radio waves
5. train station
6. a pay raise
7. favorite flavor
8. April, May
9. paid vacation
10. straight this way
11. they made mistakes
12. famous name

Exercise 17: Production

Practice pronouncing the following sentences.

1. Stay away for eight days?
2. Your pronunciation is amazing.
3. Be more patient today.
4. They need to save face.

PRETEST D

Put a check next to the words that have the /uw/ sound, as in "you."

1. _____ school
2. _____ shut
3. _____ group
4. _____ women
5. _____ future
6. _____ good
7. _____ students
8. _____ know
9. _____ through
10. _____ lose

Part IV: /uw/

(a) **do**	This is the highest back vowel, and like the other tense vowels of English, it is not pure. It begins with a pure /u/ sound but is finished with a /w/.
(b) **food**	
(c) **suit**	
(d) **soup**	The lips round into a very small circle for this sound.
(e) **use**	There are various spellings for /uw/: **oo, o, u, ue, ou, ew, ui.**
(f) **new**	

Exercise 18: Listening

You will hear a pair of words. Circle if they are the same or different.

   1. same   different

   2. same   different

   3. same   different

   4. same   different

   5. same   different

Check your answers.

   6. same   different

   7. same   different

   8. same   different

   9. same   different

10. same   different

Exercise 19: Listening

You will hear three words. Two words will have the /uw/ sound and one will be different. Put an X on the blank for the word that is different.

       1   **2**   **3**

   1. _____ _____ _____

   2. _____ _____ _____

   3. _____ _____ _____

   4. _____ _____ _____

   5. _____ _____ _____

Check your answers.

   6. _____ _____ _____

   7. _____ _____ _____

8. _____ _____ _____

9. _____ _____ _____

10. _____ _____ _____

Exercise 20: Listening

Look at the following word groups. Two words in each group will have the vowel sound /uw/ in the first syllable and one will be different. Put a check next to the word that has a different vowel sound.

1. _____ push   _____ prove   _____ pool

2. _____ youth   _____ music   _____ nothing

3. _____ around   _____ through   _____ jewelry

4. _____ juice   _____ lucky   _____ moving

5. _____ hundred   _____ human   _____ fuel

Now you will hear these words. Check your answers.

ARTICULATION

To form /uw/:

Tongue position: low   middle   (high)

front   center   (back)

Face, jaw, and tongue: tense

Mouth position: lips tightly rounded

Sound focus: (Close your eyes.) Pull your tongue high up and far back in your mouth. Round your lips tightly. Begin the /u/ sound. At the end of it, pull your tongue back a little further and push your lips a little more forward into an even tighter "o" to make /w/.

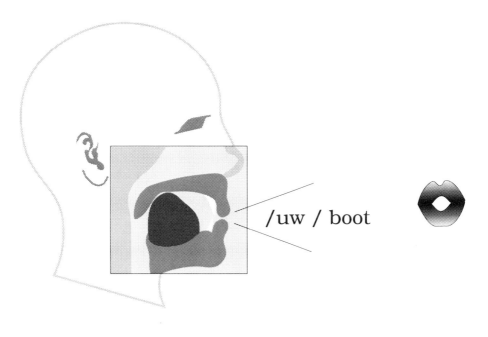

/uw / boot

Exercise 21: Production

Practice pronouncing the following words.

1. duty	6. useful	11. blue
2. moving	7. foolish	12. you
3. through	8. usual	13. excuse
4. attitude	9. who	14. Tuesday
5. beautiful	10. group	15. student

Exercise 22: Production

Practice pronouncing the following phrases.

1. fruit juice	8. a pool cue
2. a soup spoon	9. music studio
3. true blue	10. the student newspaper
4. school uniform	11. chew your food
5. cool as a cucumber	12. smooth move
6. a loose screw	13. new shoes
7. a tube of toothpaste	14. hula hoop

Exercise 23: Production

Practice pronouncing the following sentences.

1. Do you feel blue?
2. Who was that student?
3. What was your excuse for Tuesday?
4. You seem to be moving through it quickly.

PRETEST E

Put a check next to the words that have the /ow/ sound, as in "go."

1. _____ wrote   6. _____ both

2. _____ brother   7. _____ won't

3. _____ show   8. _____ coat

4. _____ own   9. _____ soak

5. _____ stone   10. _____ gone

Part V: /ow/

(a) n**o**	The /ow/ sound is a tense, mid-back vowel. Many languages use the shorter, pure /o/, but the English /ow/ is longer. It has an /o/ followed by a glide up into a /w/.
(b) m**o**st	
(c) br**o**ke	
(d) sn**ow**	
(e) b**oa**t	Some common spellings for the sound are **o, ow, oa.**

Exercise 24: Listening

You will hear a pair of words. Circle if they are the same or different.

1. same   different   4. same   different

2. same   different   5. same   different

3. same   different

Check your answers.

6. same   different

7. same   different

8. same   different

9. same   different

10. same   different

Exercise 25: Listening

You will hear three words. Two words will have the /ow/ sound and one will be different. Put an X on the blank for the word that is different.

	1	2	3
1.	_____	_____	_____
2.	_____	_____	_____
3.	_____	_____	_____
4.	_____	_____	_____
5.	_____	_____	_____

Check your answers.

6.	_____	_____	_____
7.	_____	_____	_____
8.	_____	_____	_____
9.	_____	_____	_____
10.	_____	_____	_____

Exercise 26: Listening

Look at the following word groups. Two words in each group will have the vowel sound /ow/ in the first syllable and one will be different. Put a check next to the word that has a different vowel sound.

1. _____ program   _____ colder   _____ some

2. _____ problem   _____ clothes   _____ don't

3. _____ load   _____ town   _____ window

4. _____ through   _____ comb   _____ donut

5. _____ dog   _____ oldest   _____ motion

Now you will hear these words. Check your answers.

ARTICULATION

To form /ow/:

Tongue position: low   (middle)   high

                   front   center   (back)

Face, jaw, and tongue: tense

Mouth position: lips rounded

Sound focus: (Close your eyes.) Move your tongue to about mid-position in back, open your mouth halfway, and round your lips to make the /o/ part of the sound. Then pull your tongue further up and back. Round the lips more to make the glide into /w/.

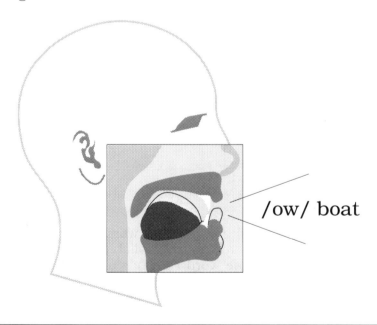

/ow/ boat

Exercise 27: Production

Practice pronouncing the following words.

1. show	6. won't	11. both
2. hotel	7. home	12. phone
3. ocean	8. postpone	13. moment
4. coal	9. alone	14. clothes
5. smoke	10. stolen	15. open

Exercise 28: Production

Practice pronouncing the following phrases.

1. cold shoulder	8. hold the phone
2. donut hole	9. no smoking
3. own a boat	10. yellow overcoat
4. told you so	11. old clothes
5. slow motion	12. rope tow
6. don't go home	13. so totally alone
7. talk show host	14. with only a moment's notice

Exercise 29: Production

Practice pronouncing the following sentences.

1. I told you so.
2. They postponed it a moment ago.
3. Don't go it alone.
4. He won't give you the cold shoulder.

See Appendix C for practice with contrasting vowels.

4

Troublesome Consonants

PRETEST A

Circle the word you hear.

1. Sue   zoo
2. face   faze
3. sap   zap
4. place   plays
5. fuss   fuzz
6. bussed   buzzed
7. muscle   muzzle
8. hiss   his

Part I: **/s/ and /z/**

		In English, there are voiced and voiceless sounds. The difference between the sounds /s/ and /z/, for example, is simply whether they are voiced or not. /z/ is voiced, and /s/ is not.
(a) place	/s/	
(b) plays	/z/	Voicing occurs when the vocal cords vibrate. If there is no vibration, we call the sound voiceless.
(c) rice	/s/	
(d) rise	/z/	All vowels are voiced. Put your hand on your throat. Say "ahhhhhhhhh" (as if during a doctor's exam). You should be able to feel a vibration.

Exercise 1: Listening

You will hear a pair of words. Circle if they are the same or different.

1. same   different

2. same   different

3. same   different

4. same   different

5. same   different

6. same   different

Exercise 2: Listening

You will hear three words. Two words will be the same and one will be different. Put an X on the blank for the word that is different.

	1	2	3
1.	_____	_____	_____
2.	_____	_____	_____
3.	_____	_____	_____
4.	_____	_____	_____

Check your answers.

5. _____   _____   _____

6. _____   _____   _____

7. _____   _____   _____

8. _____   _____   _____

ARTICULATION

To form /s/ and /z/:

Tongue position: tip under bump behind upper front teeth (not touching)
tongue pointed and curved slightly up

Sound focus: (Close your eyes.) Feel the area behind your front upper teeth with your tongue. Pull your tongue slightly back. You will feel a bump behind your teeth. Curve and point your tongue slightly up. Place it under the bump—close but not touching.

For /s/, there should be no vibration when air is released. For /z/, the vocal cords need to vibrate.

Exercise 3: Production /s/

Practice pronouncing the following words.

1. sick	6. us	11. science
2. summer	7. ask	12. stop
3. send	8. sex	13. crisis
4. this	9. step	14. cereal
5. mess	10. six	15. myself

Exercise 4: Production

Practice pronouncing the following phrases.

1. this mess	4. dance step
2. last summer	5. several stops
3. science center	6. satisfy myself

Exercise 5: Production

Practice pronouncing the following sentences.

1. Stop this bus.
2. Sue looks skinny.
3. That's some success!
4. Sam disappeared.

Exercise 6: Production /z/

Practice pronouncing the following words.

1. is	6. as	11. close
2. has	7. says	12. clothes
3. was	8. those	13. razor
4. does	9. zoo	14. lose
5. goes	10. zipper	15. noise

Exercise 7: Production

Practice pronouncing the following sentences.

1. Is the quiz easy?
2. Close those, not these.
3. Zip your zipper.
4. She does what she says.

Exercise 8: Production /s/ and /z/

Part A: Practice pronouncing the following pairs of words.

1. zoo	Sue
2. advice	advise
3. sip	zip
4. lose	loose
5. mace	maze
6. sewn	zone
7. loss	laws
8. his	hiss

Part B: Dictate one word from each pair to a partner. Compare the answers.

Part II: th /θ/ *and* /ð/

(a)	think	/θ/	**th** has 2 sounds: voiced and voiceless. You will see these symbols in pronunciation books:
(b)	this	/ð/	
(c)	nothing	/θ/	/ð/ (voiced) /θ/ (voiceless)
(d)	truth	/θ/	This can be a very uncomfortable sound to make because you will need to put your tongue out a bit.
(e)	father	/ð/	

ARTICULATION

To form /th/:

Tongue position: Flat. Let it lightly touch the top and bottom teeth. It should stick out a little so you can see it in a mirror.

Sound focus: (Close your eyes.) Run the tip of your tongue over your top and bottom teeth. Gently bite the tip of your tongue. Slightly release it. Force the air out. There should be friction. Don't pull your tongue in as you make this sound.

For /θ/, there should be no vocal cord vibration. It is voiceless.

For /ð/, the vocal cords need to vibrate. Put your hand on your throat to feel the vibration.

Exercise 9: Production /θ/

Practice pronouncing the following words.

1. think
2. thin
3. worth
4. thank
5. thorough
6. theme
7. math
8. thing
9. wealthy
10. both

Exercise 10: Production /ð/

Same as before.

1. this	6. weather
2. that	7. whether
3. these	8. father
4. those	9. bathe
5. there	10. mother

Exercise 11: Production

Practice pronouncing the following phrases.

1. these things
2. wealthy father
3. this math text
4. the weather report
5. something on Thursday
6. thank your mother
7. a thousand theories
8. nothing worth thinking about

Exercise 12: Production

Practice pronouncing the following sentences.

1. That's nothing.
2. Did you say north or south?
3. This month is colder than last month.
4. I thought you thought that through.

Exercise 13: Production (Optional)

Practice pronouncing the following tongue twister.

> Theophilus Thistle, the successful thistle sifter, while sifting a sifter of unsifted thistles, thrust three-thousand thistles through the thick of his thumb.*

*Source unknown.

PRETEST B (/r/ AND /l/)

Circle the word you hear.

1. fair   fail

2. rice   lice

3. read   lead

4. mare   mail

5. car   call

Check your answers.

6. crowd   cloud

7. berry   belly

8. boring   bowling

9. rung   lung

10. fire   file

Part III: /r/ and /l/

(a) red (b) right (c) lead (d) light (e) real (f) library	/r/ and /l/ are very similar in some languages. This can make them very hard to hear. If you don't have these sounds in your language, they will be difficult to learn. Don't give up! Practice every day. After several **months**, they will be easier to hear and pronounce.

Exercise 14: Listening

You will hear a pair of words. Circle if they are the same or different.

1. same   different

2. same   different

3. same   different

4. same   different

5. same   different

Check your answers.

6. same   different

7. same   different

8. same   different

9. same   different

10. same   different

Exercise 15: Listening

You will hear three words. Two will have the sound /r/ or /l/ and one will be different. Put an X on the line for the word that is different.

	1	2	3
1.			
2.			
3.			
4.			
5.			

Check your answers.

6.			
7.			
8.			
9.			
10.			

ARTICULATION

To form /r/:

Tongue tip: slightly curved up toward the hard palate
it should NOT be touching anything

Sides of tongue: touch against molar teeth (tightly to
make sure air will not escape there)

Sound focus: (Close your eyes.) Rest your tongue flat on the
bottom of your mouth. RELAX it. Raise it up. Let the sides
touch the back molar teeth. Run the sides against them and
rest there. The tip should be slightly curved but not touching.

Tip: Say "ahhhhhh." While you are saying this, press your
cheeks in with your fingers. This will form /r/.

Exercise 16: Production

Practice pronouncing the following words.

1. write	6. marry	11. around
2. rent	7. over	12. weird
3. rib	8. wreck	13. react
4. secretary	9. where	14. reason
5. read	10. understand	15. refrigerator

Exercise 17: Production

Practice pronouncing the following phrases.

1. red hair	4. weird reaction
2. four hours	5. weather report
3. right reason	6. read over

Exercise 18: Production /ar/

To form /ar/, make the /a/ sound. Remember that your tongue is
low and flat. Slowly curl the tip of your tongue back to /r/ position.
Don't open your mouth very much at all when you make the /a/
sound, and /r/ will be easier to form. (Hint: Some students have an
easier time making this sound if they smile a bit.)

Practice pronouncing the following words. (Come back to this exercise as many times as necessary.)

1. car	6. heart	11. card
2. far	7. start	12. remark
3. dark	8. farther*	13. bar
4. arm	9. hard	14. smart
5. partner	10. carpet	15. art

Exercise 19: Production /ər/

To form /ər/, begin with your tongue in the /ə/ position. Move it higher, and then slowly take it back to the /r/ position.

Practice pronouncing the following words. (Come back to this exercise as many times as necessary.)

1. her	6. we're†	11. bird
2. were	7. person	12. burn
3. word	8. murder	13. purple
4. girl	9. shirt	14. pearl
5. work	10. hamburger	15. early

Exercise 20: Production

Part A: Comparisons are good practice for the /ər/ ending. Practice pronouncing the following words.

1. cheap	cheaper
2. big	bigger
3. hard	harder
4. deep	deeper
5. smart	smarter
6. near	nearer
7. fat	fatter
8. hot	hotter

Part B: Choose six of the comparative forms that you have just practiced. Write one question for each. Then interview a native speaker and write his/her answers. Example: "Which is harder for you: English or Math?" Report your answers to the class.

*Compare with "father."   †relaxed pronunciation

Exercise 21: Production /ar/ and /ər/

Practice pronouncing the following sentences.

1. Those were her words.
2. You're sure here early.
3. It's hard to learn.
4. Park the car near the market.
5. I heard it's far.

Exercise 22: Production — /r/ Review

Practice pronouncing the following sentences.

1. Where were you?
2. Read the report for Thursday.
3. You're neither right nor wrong.
4. We were there four hours.

ARTICULATION

To form /l/:

Tongue tip: curved up, touching the tooth ridge.

Sides of tongue: do NOT touch anything.

Sound focus: (Close your eyes.) Run the tip of your tongue over the tooth ridge. Let it rest on the bump behind your teeth. The rest of your tongue should not be touching anything. When you release your tongue, let it move slightly forward—don't pull it down. (For final /l/, keep your tongue on the bump. Let the sound fade.)

Exercise 23: Production

Practice pronouncing the following words.

1. last	5. meal	9. mail	13. feeling
2. like	6. list	10. feel	14. ugly
3. sell	7. nail	11. lost	15. ballet
4. love	8. mall	12. ball	

Exercise 24: Production

Practice pronouncing the following phrases.

1. really late
2. lazy lunch
3. love letter
4. ugly feeling
5. full meal
6. feel like

Exercise 25: Production

Practice pronouncing the following sentences.

1. I feel like lunch.
2. I was at the law library late.
3. You don't look well.
4. Can you change a dollar bill?

Exercise 26: Production

Part A: Practice pronouncing the following pairs of words.

1. rain   lane
2. male   mare
3. peel   peer
4. feel   fear
5. wrist   list
6. Ross   loss
7. prod   plod
8. all   are

Part B: Dictate one word from each pair to a partner. Compare the answers.

Exercise 27: Production

Practice pronouncing the following sentences with /r/ and /l/.

1. I ordered a world atlas.
2. Show me your credit card.
3. There's a special rate for a round-trip ticket.
4. It's a common word in our vocabulary book.

Exercise 28: Production

Same as before.

1. I heard my car alarm.
2. Practice makes perfect.
3. What's the problem?
4. Your refrigerator's leaking water.

Part IV: Nonreleased Final Consonants

(a) sto<u>p</u>	/p/	One of the more difficult problems in learning to pronounce correctly is nonreleased final consonants. When the sounds:
(b) hate	/t/	/p/, /t/, /k/, /b/, /d/, /g/
(c) sna<u>ck</u>	/k/	come at the end of a word, the sound is formed but not released. *Closure* is made, but the sound is not released. (Closure is when the vowel sound is stopped by a consonant). Compare the following:
(d) Bo<u>b</u>	/b/	
(e) sa<u>d</u>	/d/	
(f) bi<u>g</u>	/g/	day/date
		sew/sewed
(g) cab/cap		You will notice that the vowels before the voiced sounds /b/, /d/, and /g/ are *longer*. It is very important when pronouncing words ENDING with /b/, /d/, and /g/ that you lengthen the vowel.
(h) hat/had		
(i) duck/dug		If you compare (g), (h), and (i), you will see that it is hard to tell the difference in the endings. However, you can hear a longer vowel in each pair.
(j) He's back. *He's bag.		When you are listening to these words, context will help you recognize the correct meaning.

*Not English.

Exercise 29: Listening

Listen to the following pairs of words. Note the closure. Remember that when the word ends with a voiced consonant, the vowel is longer.

1. day	date	6. birthday	birthdate
2. feed	feet	7. lead	Lee
3. dope	doe	8. mop	mob
4. goat	go	9. stayed	state
5. slow	slope	10. babe	bay

Exercise 30: Listening

Listen to the following sentences. Notice the final sound.

1. He is late.
2. I gained some weight.
3. Maybe I could.
4. What was that about?
5. Stop that cab.
6. We learned those by heart.
7. I need a plastic bag.
8. I asked* for a little bit.

Exercise 31: Listening

You will hear a pair of words. Circle if they are the same or different.

1. same   different

2. same   different

3. same   different

4. same   different

5. same   different

6. same   different

*æst

Exercise 32: Listening

Circle "yes" if you hear a final consonant and "no" if not.

1. yes   no

2. yes   no

3. yes   no

4. yes   no

5. yes   no

6. yes   no

Exercise 33: Production

Listen to the following pairs of words. Notice the difference in vowel length. Remember, the final consonants /b/, /d/, and /g/ are voiced, and you will need to make the vowels before them longer.

1. dock   dog
2. mat   mad
3. pick   pig
4. let   led
5. mop   mob
6. rip   rib
7. at   add

Practice pronouncing these pairs of words.

Exercise 34: Production

Practice pronouncing the following sentences. Remember that the final consonants in the italicized words are not released.

1. I *forgot.*
2. *Nope!* That's *not right.*
3. It's too *big.*
4. *Take* 10 minutes.
5. This test looks way too *hard.*
6. *Did* she *rob that* store?
7. I'm *mad.*
8. I want your *birthdate*, not *birthday.*

Exercise 35: Dictation

Choose ten words from the chapter that are difficult for you. Write them below. Dictate them to a partner or native speaker. Compare answers when you are finished.

1.   6.

2.   7.

3.   8.

4.   9.

5.   10.

Part V: Consonant Clusters

(a) strengths /str ... nkθs/ (b) charged / ... rjd/ (c) thrift /θr ... ft/ (d) government / ... rnm ... nt/ (e) sixths / ... ksθs/ (f) squirrel /skw ... rl/	English syllables can have as many as **three** consonant sounds before the vowel. As many as **four** consonants can follow it. (a) shows you examples of both. Most languages do not have groups of consonants (called **consonant clusters**). Therefore, pronouncing consonant clusters is not easy for many nonnative speakers.
strike: /strayk/ (native speaker pronunciation)	In trying to make consonant clusters easier to pronounce, nonnative speakers generally make the following kinds of errors:
(g) /sətərayə/ (typical of Japanese speakers) (h) /ɛstrayk/ (typical of Spanish speakers)	(1) inserting extra vowel sounds in front of, between, or after consonants in the cluster, as in (g) and (h).
(i) /stayk/ or /tayk/	(2) omitting some of the consonant sounds to shorten the cluster, as in (i).*

*Native speakers sometimes leave out consonants in clusters, too, but they do it in ways that don't interfere with understanding. See Chapter 11, "Reductions in Consonant Clusters."

Exercise 36: Listening and Production

Listen as the following pairs of words are pronounced. The first word of each pair has a vowel between the underlined consonants, and has two syllables. The second word of the pair has a consonant cluster and only one syllable. Practice pronouncing the pairs.

1. parade	prayed	6. licit	list
2. polite	plight	7. granite	grant
3. collapse	claps	8. pellet	pelt
4. below	blow	9. support	sport
5. rigid	ridged	10. cassock	cask

Exercise 37: Listening and Production

Listen as the following pairs of words are pronounced. The first word in each pair has a short vowel sound at the beginning. The second word does not; it begins with an *s*-consonant cluster. Practice pronouncing the pairs.

1. aspire	spire	5. asleep	sleep
2. escape	scape	6. esteem	steam
3. astir	stir	7. astride	stride
4. estate	state	8. esprit	spree

Exercise 38: Production

Pronounce each word carefully. Concentrate on the /s/ sound, and, if you need to, lengthen it to avoid making a vowel sound before it.

1. speak	6. scream
2. smoking	7. split
3. snowy	8. school
4. sleep	9. sweater
5. square	10. stretch

Exercise 39: Production

Pronounce each word carefully. Be sure to articulate each consonant in the clusters that are underlined. If you need to, slow down your speed and exaggerate the pronunciation of each consonant so that you can feel them clearly. Then pronounce the words again at a more normal speed. Be careful not to add extra vowel sounds.

1. fl̲y	6. s̲h̲rink
2. bul̲b̲	7. taxe̲d̲
3. s̲n̲eeze	8. film̲e̲d̲
4. p̲r̲oud	9. instructions
5. fin̲d̲	10. s̲top̲p̲e̲d̲

If you are having trouble with **consonant clusters** at the beginning of words, the following exercise will give you more practice.

Exercise 40: Production

There are 47 different combinations of two or three consonants that can come at the beginning of a syllable!* One way to practice is to build from one consonant to two- and three- consonant clusters. Practice pronouncing the following words. Be careful not to add extra vowels as you add consonants.

1. mall, small	7. red, thread
2. lie, fly	8. rate, trait, straight
3. no, snow	9. rip, trip, strip
4. wick, quick	10. rain, train, strain
5. led, bled	11. ride, tried, stride
6. you, cue	12. lay, play, splay

The following exercise will give you more practice with clusters at the ends of words.

Exercise 41: Production

There are 169 different combinations of two, three, or four consonants that can end a syllable! The most common are clusters with two consonants, especially /nt/ and /ts/.† Because these endings are important for meaning, they must be pronounced and cannot be omitted.

Pronounce the following groups of words. Be careful of the clusters that are made when the **-s**, **-ed**, and **-th** endings are added.

*Adapted from Prator and Robinett (1985). *Manual of American English Pronunciation* (4th ed.). New York: Holt, Rinehart and Winston.
†Ibid., pp. 175, 177–178.

1. like, likes, liked
2. miss, missed
3. wash, washed
4. nine, ninth, ninths
5. seven, seventh, sevenths

6. warm, warmth, warms, warmed
7. curl, curls, curled
8. help, helps, helped
9. were, word, world, worlds
10. change, changed

Part VI: Consonant Combinations in Phrases and Sentences

(a) **sounds gr**eat /..ndzgr../

(b) **Fir**st **Str**eet /..rststr../

(c) mi**nced squ**ash /..ntstskw../

So far, we have been looking at clusters in single words. But in connected speech, it is easy to find combinations of five, six, and sometimes even seven consonants in a row, as in (a)–(c).

Exercise 42: Listening and Production

Part A: Listen as the following short sequences of words are pronounced. Notice how the last consonant sound of the cluster in each first word is pronounced as if it were the first consonant in the following word.

1. weird answer
2. stopped it
3. moved in
4. start over
5. lots of
6. arranged everything
7. don't ask
8. washed up

Part B: Practice pronouncing these phrases.

Chapter 5, "Linking" will give you more practice with clusters in phrases and sentences.

For explanations of and practice with the other consonants, see Appendix A, "Consonant Practice," and Appendix B, "Minimal Pair Practice with Consonants."

5

Linking

Part I: Linking with Vowels

a. That's enough.

b. Why am I this busy?

c. Have a seat.

d. It's an interesting idea.

When a word begins with a vowel, the consonant(s) from the word before is moved over. This is called **linking**.

In usual speech, English has a consonant-vowel (CV) pattern. Linking lets speakers keep this pattern.

Exercise 1: Listening

Listen to the following sentences. Mark the linking.

1. It's over in an hour.

2. Care for anything else?

3. I'll be in* in ten minutes.

4. Let's leave in another hour.

5. Can I do* it?

6. I'm taking a one-hour break.

*Advanced students may notice a /y/ or /w/ sound, respectively, linking these two words. For more information, please refer to the Teacher's Manual.

Exercise 2: Listening

Fill in the blanks with the words you hear.

1. I do this _____.

2. It's _____.

3. Let's leave _____.

4. _____ being called?

5. Was your _____ tea?

Check your answers.

6. It's _____.

7. That's _____ for now.

8. Please _____.

9. It's time _____ break.

10. You look _____ you're tired.

Exercise 3: Production

Mark the linking in the following phrases. Practice pronouncing them.

1. off and on   6. now or never

2. all over   7. that's all

3. in an hour   8. come again

4. am I   9. for a

5. coffee or tea   10. as if

Exercise 4: Production

Mark the linking. Practice pronouncing the following sentences.

1. I do this off and on.

2. It's all over.

3. Let's leave in an hour.

4. Am I being called?

5. Was your order coffee or tea?

Exercise 5: Production

Same as before.

1. It's now or never.

2. That's all for now.

3. Please come again.

4. It's time for a relaxing evening.

5. You look as if you're tired.

Exercise 6: Listening and Production (Review)

Part A: Listen to the following sentences. Mark the linking.

1. The talk lasts another hour.

2. When am I expected?

3. If it's O.K., we're leaving.

4. That was an expensive accident.

5. I wish I could.

Part B: Practice pronouncing these sentences.

Exercise 7: Listening and Production (Optional)

Same as before.

1. Tell me again how it works.

2. The movie ends in a half-hour.

3. Sooner or later I may ask.

4. It's due in eleven days.

5. Try again in a few minutes.

Part II: Linking Identical Consonants

a. bad day

b. at two

c. unusual life

d. next time

When the end of one word has the same sound as the beginning of the next, the words are **linked**. The final sound of the first word is formed but used for the following word.

Exercise 8: Production

Mark the linking. Practice pronouncing the following phrases.

1. put together
2. with that
3. next Tuesday
4. been no
5. over real

6. next time
7. guess some
8. finish shopping
9. good deal
10. this sound

Exercise 9: Production

Mark the linking. Practice pronouncing the following sentences.

1. This sound is difficult.
2. It's over real* early.
3. There's a party next Tuesday.
4. Are you through with that?
5. I guess some people like it.

*Informal English

I guess some people like it.

Exercise 10: Production (Optional)

Same as before.

1. When will you finish shopping?

2. There's a good deal more available.

3. Next time will be a little different.

4. Put together one for me.

5. There's been no time.

CHAPTER REVIEW

Exercise 11: Dialogue Practice

Practice the following dialogues with a partner. Before you read your sentence, study it for a moment so that when you speak, you can look at your partner without reading. Also, mark the linking.

1. *A:* Take a seat.

   B: Over here or over there?

2. *A:* Care for anything else?

   B: I'm all done, thanks.

3. *A:* That's all for now.

   B: I'm glad it's over.

4. *A:* Did you want coffee or tea?

   B: Either's O.K.

5. *A:* Next time, come early.

   B: I could do that.

Exercise 12: Paragraph Reading

Read the following paragraph aloud. Before you begin, make sure you understand all the vocabulary. Ask your teacher or check your dictionary. Also, mark where you think words will be linked, and put slash marks (/) where you think you should pause. (Pauses occur after grammatical chunks, often marked by punctuation.)

Greetings

In North America, when people greet each other, they

generally say, "Hi, how are you?" This is NOT a question

but rather a greeting. The expected answer is usually

short, for example:

"Fine"

"O.K."

"Pretty good"

"Not bad"

A long, detailed answer or a negative answer would be

strange unless you knew the person very well and could

tell that the person expected more extensive information.

People learning English may think that native speakers

are impolite because they do not stop to have a conversation. But "How are you?" should be thought of in the same way as "Hello." It's simply a greeting.

Exercise 13: Short Presentation

Study the following information. Using your own words, put together a short, one-minute talk about the various ways to cook meat and eggs, or, how you like to have them cooked. You can refer to your notes, but don't read them as you speak. Your teacher will choose one aspect (part) of pronunciation for you to focus on. (Note: this is good practice for /r/ and /l/.)

Meat and Eggs: Getting Them Cooked Right in a Restaurant

In restaurants, when you order meat or eggs, you will usually be asked how you want them cooked. Following are the more common terms for ordering:

Meat

rare: red inside

medium rare: red in the middle, not all through

medium: pink

well-done: cooked a lot, not pink inside

Eggs

scrambled: beaten and then fried

soft-boiled

hard-boiled

poached: steamed or lightly boiled out of the shell

fried

    sunnyside up: cooked on one side only, the yolk (yellow part) is not cooked on top

    over easy: cooked on both sides, but the yolk is very lightly cooked

    over medium: cooked on both sides, and the white covering of the yolk is not runny

    hard: the yolk is cooked.

Exercise 14: Picture Description

Say as much as you can about the picture in one minute.

Exercise 15: Production (Optional)

Go back to Chapter 4. Mark the linking for the sentences in exercises 5, 7, 12, 21, 22, 25, 27 and 28. Practice pronouncing them.

6

Consonant Replacements

Part I: The Flap

(a) water (b) medical	When t or d occurs between vowels, a sound called the "flap" is produced. This sound is similar to a /d/, but much faster. The tongue tip touches the tooth ridge very quickly.
(c) right away (d) what if (e) I've got to go.	Linking makes the flap very common. Many words, when spoken alone, do not have flaps (e.g., "what," "that"). However, when linked, as in (c), (d), and (e), a flap can be formed.
(f) that'll (g) You hurt it.	Between a vowel and /l/ or /r/, the t may sound like a /d/.

Exercise 1: Listening

Listen for the flap or /d/ in the following words.

1. letter
2. model
3. bottle
4. middle
5. butter
6. better
7. settle
8. bitter
9. that'll
10. idiom

Exercise 2: Listening

Listen for the flap or /d/ in the following phrases and mark the linking.

1. what if
2. tired out
3. right away
4. put it
5. got to

6. at all
7. what about it
8. forget it
9. what I
10. at eight

Exercise 3: Production

Practice pronouncing the following words and phrases.

1. letter
2. what if
3. put it
4. middle
5. at all

6. got to
7. better
8. that'll
9. idiom
10. right away

Exercise 4: Production

Same as before.

1. bottle
2. bitter
3. ought to
4. better
5. model

6. what I
7. water
8. tired out
9. what about
10. put out

Exercise 5: What are you/What do you

Native speakers often pronounce "What are you" and "What do you" as "Whaddaya." The d̲ is a flap.

Part A: Listen to the following sentences.

1. What are you thinking?   What do you think?
2. What are you spending?   What do you spend?
3. What are you eating?   What do you eat?

4. What are you paying?   What do you pay?

5. What are you taking?   What do you take?

Part B: Practice pronouncing the above phrases with a partner.

Part II: The Glottal Stop

(a) I've eaten.	*ea'n*	When t is followed by the syllable /n/, many native speakers use a special sound, called a glottal stop, to replace the t. A glottal stop is formed when the vocal cords close completely for a moment, stopping the air. You hear this sound in the negative expression "uh uh."
(b) He's certain.	*cer'n*	
(c) It's written down.	*wri'n*	
(d) Something isn't right.	*su'm*	Note the special pronunciation for "something."
		The symbol you often see in pronunciation books for a glottal stop is /ʔ/.

Exercise 6: Listening

Fill in the blanks with the words you hear.

1. I need white _____ pants.

2. What have you _____ today?

3. It's a difficult _____ to pronounce.

4. Don't order such _____ food.

5. It's _____ late.

Check your answers.

6. You need three _____ eggs.

7. _____ wrong with this chair.

8. _____ things don't make sense.

9. Use an empty milk _____.

10. I'd like to get a _____ bike.

Exercise 7: Production

Practice pronouncing the following words.

1. fattening		6. gotten
2. cotton		7. beaten
3. eaten		8. mountain
4. sentence		9. certain
5. something		10. carton

Exercise 8: Production

With a partner, practice pronouncing the following phrases.

1. cotton pants	6. beaten egg
2. getting late	7. something's wrong
3. difficult sentence	8. certain things
4. fattening food	9. milk carton
5. eaten already	10. mountain bike

Part III: Can/Can't

(a) I can see.	I *kn* see.	In the affirmative, "can" is un-stressed. The main verb is stressed (except if "can" is at the end of a phrase).
(b) She can come.	She *kn* come.	
(c) They can tell.	They *kn* tell.	
(d) I can't see.	I *KAN'* see.	In the negative form, both "can't" and the main verb are stressed. The t in "can't," however, is dropped and the final sound is pronounced as a glottal stop.*
(e) She can't come.	She *KAN'* come.	
(f) They can't tell.	They *KAN'* tell.	

*This occurs when the next sound is a consonant. If it is a vowel, there will be a flap, as in "We can't accept that."

Exercise 9: Listening

Listen to the following sentences.

1. Can we drive there?
2. I can't* understand that.

*Remember, a flap is pronounced here.

3. You can come later.
4. How can that be?
5. What can be done?
6. It can't be done over.
7. That can't be right.
8. We can try again.

How can that be?

Exercise 10: Listening

Circle the word you hear.

1. can   can't
2. can   can't
3. can   can't
4. can   can't
5. can   can't

Check your answers.

6. can   can't
7. can   can't
8. can   can't
9. can   can't
10. can   can't

Exercise 11: Listening (Optional)

Fill in the blanks with the words you hear.

1. Where _____ I find it?

2. _____ you work late tonight?

3. I _____ reach her.

4. That _____ happen anytime.

5. When _____ you come?

Check your answers.

6. _____ you help more?

7. They _____ be a problem.

8. I _____ see a thing.

9. You _____ get one cheap.

10. _____ that be done?

Exercise 12: Production

Practice pronouncing the following sentences. Focus on the "can"/ "can't" contrast.

1. Can we help?
2. I can't understand.
3. You can come.
4. How can that be?
5. What can be done?
6. It can't be helped.

Exercise 13: Production

With a partner, complete the sentences with a verb of your choice. Practice pronouncing the sentences.

1. That can't . . .
2. We can . . .
3. It can't . . .
4. When can you . . .

5. Why can't she . . .
6. How can they . . .

Exercise 14: Production (Optional)

Make a list of what you can/can't do in your host country. Compare it to your country. Tell the class about it.

1.   5.

2.   6.

3.   7.

4.   8.

Part IV: Negative Contractions

(a) You wouldn't do that.	*wouldn'*	Many speakers don't pronounce the final t in a negative contraction. Rather, they make a glottal stop.
(b) That couldn't work.	*couldn'*	
(c) I haven't seen it.	*haven'*	
(d) Don't do that.	*don'*	

Exercise 15: Listening

Listen to the following sentences.

1. That doesn't work.
2. You wouldn't believe it.
3. I hadn't thought that.
4. Shouldn't they be here?
5. We didn't know.
6. That doesn't matter.
7. I haven't got time.
8. She couldn't do that.

Exercise 16: Production

Practice pronouncing the following phrases.

1. doesn't work
2. wouldn't believe
3. hadn't thought

4. shouldn't they
5. didn't know
6. doesn't matter
7. haven't got
8. couldn't do

Exercise 17: Production

Write six sentences (negative contraction + verb). Practice pronouncing them and then dictate them to a partner. Compare the sentences.

1.

2.

3.

4.

5.

6.

Exercise 18: Production

With a partner, practice pronouncing the following pairs of sentences.

1. Who would know?   Who wouldn't know?
2. She does want to.   She doesn't want to.
3. I could help.   I couldn't help.
4. They have got time.   They haven't got time.
5. Should she be here?   Shouldn't she be here?
6. That did make sense.   That didn't make sense.

CHAPTER REVIEW

Exercise 19: Dialogue Practice

Practice the following dialogues with a partner. Before you say your sentence, study it for a moment so that when you speak, you can look at your partner without reading. Mark the linking and where you think the sounds might change. Remember to focus on the flap, glottal stop, and can/can't.

1. *A:* What do you want?

   B: I can't decide.

2. *A:* Forget everything I said.

   B: I did already.

3. *A:* What about getting some dinner?

   B: I've got to do something else.

4. *A:* This ought to taste great.

   B: Everything fattening does!

5. *A:* Can you pick me up at eight?

   B: I can come even earlier.

6. *A:* How come you weren't there?

   B: I couldn't get a ride.

Exercise 20: Sentence Completion

With a partner, finish the sentences with words of your choice. (Keep them short.) Before you say your sentence, study it for a moment so that when you speak, you can look at you partner without reading. Mark the linking and where you think the sounds might change. Remember to focus on the flap, glottal stop, and can/can't.

1. What I need is . . .

2. Certain people . . .

3. I can't remember . . .

4. What if I . . .

5. I shouldn't . . .

6. I'm getting . . .

7. I think something's . . .

8. That'll make me . . .

Exercise 21: Paragraph Reading

Read the following paragraph aloud. Before you begin, make sure you understand all the vocabulary. Ask your teacher or check your dictionary. Also, mark the linking and where you think the sounds might change.

A Paradox

A paradox is a statement that seems impossible because

it contradicts itself, but in fact, has some truth to it.

One of the most famous paradoxes is often studied in

logic classes. It concerns a little boy who has learned

that God can do anything. The boy is puzzled. If God

can do anything, he reasons, then can He make a rock

so big that He can't move it?!!

Exercise 22: Short Presentation

Study the following information. Using your own words, put together a short, one-minute talk about penalties for drunk driving. You can refer to your notes, but don't read them when you speak. Your teacher will choose one aspect (part) of pronunciation for you to focus on.

The High Cost of Drunk Driving

In the United States the penalties for drunk driving have become very strict in many areas. In the state of Washington, for example, if you are stopped for drunk driving the first time, you are responsible for the following costs:

1. Lawyer: $500–$1,000 minimum
2. Fines: $400–$1,600
3. Insurance: Up to $1,000/year for 3 years
4. Towing: A minimum of $50
5. Alcohol and drug evaluation test: $75
6. Getting your license back: $50

7. Alcoholism treatment (if the judge decides you need it: $1,200–$15,000)
8. Alcohol information school: $120
9. Possible lost income from required one night in jail

Total **minimum** cost: about $3,200

Exercise 23: Interview

Part A: Interview two native speakers of English. Write their answers in the blanks, and remember to have them sign their names. When asking your questions, focus especially on the negative contractions and "can." Study each question before you speak so that you do not have to read it. You may want to practice with a partner first.

1. How can a person make friends?
2. How can students best learn English?
3. What wouldn't you ever do?
4. How can people have a good time in this area?
5. When shouldn't you eat?
6. What can't you understand?
7. What can be improved in your life?
8. What subjects shouldn't be discussed?

Person #1

1.
2.
3.
4.
5.
6.
7.
8.

Person #2

1.
2.
3.
4.
5.
6.
7.
8.

_____
(signature)

_____
(signature)

Part B: Report your answers to the class or small group your teacher assigns.

Exercise 24: Picture Description

Say as much as you can about the picture in one minute.

7

Common Reductions

Part I: Reductions with /h/

(a) What has happened?	/h/ is often dropped with such function words as:
(b) If only we had known.	his have
	her has
(c) What's he want?	him had
	he

Exercise 1: Listening

Listen to the following phrases. Note the /h/ deletion.

1. if he
2. what he*
3. is her
4. that's his
5. what's her
6. should have
7. why has
8. where had
9. when her
10. could have
11. when he
12. did he*

*Remember the flap rule, Chapter 6.

Exercise 2: Listening and Production

Part A: Listen to the following phrases.

1. when he
          her
          his
          had
          has
2. did he
         her
         his
3. what's her
              his
4. what have
          has
          had
5. if he
       her
       his
6. with her
         his
         him
7. should have
   could
   would
   might

Part B: With a partner, choose some of the phrases in this exercise to practice.

Exercise 3: Listening

Fill in the blanks with the words you hear.

1. Did _____ leave?

2. When's _____ date?

3. Why _____ he come?

4. What _____ you got?

Check your answers.

5. I can't go with _____.

6. Did _____ phone call come?

7. I _____ tried that.

8. What's _____ waiting for?

Exercise 4: Listening (Optional)

Same as before.

1. That's what _____ wants.

2. Is _____ address correct?

3. That's _____ idea.

4. I wish I _____ known.

Check your answers.

5. What _____ they done?

6. When _____ she ever helped?

7. We _____ never tried that.

8. It's _____ opinion, not mine.

Exercise 5: Sentence Completion

Finish the sentences with words of your choice. (Keep them short.) Then, with a partner, practice pronouncing the sentences.

1. Did he . . .
2. When's her . . .
3. Why has . . .
4. What have . . .
5. . . . with her.
6. I could have . . .

Exercise 6: Sentence Completion (Optional)

Same as before.

1. That's what he . . .
2. Is her . . .
3. That's his . . .
4. What has . . .
5. We should have . . .
6. How has . . .

Part II: *going to/want to/have to/has to*

		In spoken English, "going to," "want to," "have to," and "has to" are reduced as follows:
(a) I'm going to leave.	*gonna*	
(b) We want to know.	*wanna*	going to → *gonna*
(c) You have to try.	*hafta*	want to → *wanna*
(d) She has to come.	*hasta*	have to → *hafta*
		has to → *hasta*

Exercise 7: Listening

Fill in the blanks with the words you hear.

1. When do you _____?
2. It's _____ soon.
3. Who _____?
4. I _____ by tomorrow.

Check your answers.

5. Everything's _____ turn out OK.
6. You _____ a better idea.
7. It _____ in when?
8. Why are they _____?

Exercise 8: Listening and Production

Listen to the following sentences. Practice pronouncing them and focus on the italicized part of each sentence.

1. *It has to* work.
2. *I want to* go.
3. *You have to* wait.
4. *Who's going to* come?
5. *She has to* know.
6. *I want to* rest.

Exercise 9: Listening and Production

Same as before.

1. *I have to know* by tomorrow.
2. *We want to try* again.
3. *What's going to* happen?
4. *When do you want to* eat?
5. *It has to be* tomorrow.
6. When are they *going to want to come*?

Exercise 10: Sentence Completion

With a partner, finish the sentences with a verb of your choice. Practice the sentences.

1. You have to . . .
2. I want to . . .
3. They have to . . .
4. Who's going to . . .
5. She has to . . .
6. You want to . . .

Exercise 11: Sentence Completion (Optional)

Same as before.

1. I have to . . .
2. We want to . . .
3. What's going to . . .

4. When do you want to . . .

5. It has to . . .

6. When are they going to want to . . .

Part III: *of*

(a) Some of them are here. some/ə/ (b) One of those looks O.K. one/ə/	"Of" is often pronounced /ə/ before a consonant.
(c) Most of us are here. most/əv/	Before a vowel, "of" is pronounced /əv/.
(d) I'm out of time.	Remember the flap rule (Chapter 6). In (d), the sound /ə/ is preceded by a flap.

Exercise 12: Listening

Listen to the following sentences. Underline the reduced phrases.

1. I'm out of money.

2. It's a waste of time.

3. One of us can do it.

4. Some of that would be O.K.

5. It's an out-of-state check.

6. I don't see the point of that.

7. All of the cars are used.

8. I can only get a dollar's worth of gas.

Exercise 13: Listening

Fill in the blanks with the words you hear.

1. _____ can go.

2. _____ shows are reruns.

3. It's an _____ license.

4. _____ looks spoiled.

I don't see the point of that.

Check your answers.

5. That project is a _____.

6. The _____ isn't clear.

7. I need a _____ change.

8. I'm running _____ patience.

Exercise 14: Production

Practice pronouncing the following phrases.

1. out of money
2. waste of time
3. one of us
4. some of that
5. out-of-state
6. point of that
7. all of the
8. dollar's worth of

Exercise 15: Listening and Production

Listen to the following sentences. Practice pronouncing them and focus on the italicized part of the sentence.

1. It looks *out of date*.
2. *Some of that* tastes bad.

3. *What of it?**
4. We're *proud of her.*
5. There's *plenty of time.*
6. I like that *best of all.*

Exercise 16: Listening and Production (Optional)

Same as before.

1. I've still got a *couple of hours.*
2. We're† not *in favor of it.*
3. They're *kind of excited.*
4. Isn't this *sort of early?*
5. I got *rid of it.*
6. We ran *out of gas.*

Exercise 17: Sentence Completion

With a partner, finish the sentences with words of your choice. (Keep them short.) Practice pronouncing the sentences.

1. A couple of hours . . .
2. One of us . . .
3. Some of that . . .
4. All of the . . .
5. I'm out of . . .
6. That's a waste of . . .

Part IV: and/or/for

(a) **Pass the salt and pepper.** (b) **Either Monday or Tuesday is O.K.** (c) **What's for dinner?**	Notice the reductions for "and," "or," and "for": and → 'n or → 'r for → *fer*

---

*This idiom is considered impolite, meaning "I don't care." Note that "of" is stressed.

†"We're" can be pronounced as the past tense "were."

Exercise 18: Listening

Fill in the blanks with the words you hear.

1. I just need to run in _____ out.

2. Let's just wait _____ see.

3. _____ once and _____ all, stop!

4. Did you say black _____ blue?

5. Look in the lost _____ found.

Exercise 19: Listening (Optional)

Same as before.

1. Did you want hard _____ soft ice-cream?

2. You'll need a suit _____ tie.

3. Did you mean Tuesday _____ Thursday?

4. We just talked about this _____ that.

5. Let's just wait _____ see.

Exercise 20: Production

Practice pronouncing the following phrases.

1. coffee or tea
2. stop and go
3. life and death
4. for now
5. yes or no
6. cash or charge
7. black and blue
8. for everyone
9. sick and tired
10. for me

Exercise 21: Listening and Production

Listen to the following sentences and practice pronouncing them. Focus especially on the italicized part of each sentence.

1. *Now and then* I take a 3-day weekend.
2. *Sooner or later* you'll get it.
3. *For the time being*, I don't have an answer.
4. It's *more or less* finished.

5. Are you *coming or going*?
6. *For once** I slept in!
7. I'm *sick and tired* of work.
8. It was *stop and go* traffic all the way.

CHAPTER REVIEW

Exercise 22: Dialogue Practice

Practice the following dialogues with a partner. Before you read your sentence, study it for a moment so that when you speak, you can look at your partner without reading.

Mark the linking and where you think the sounds might change. Remember to focus on the reductions you have studied in this chapter.

1. *A:* What's for breakfast?

   B: Potatoes and eggs and coffee.

2. *A:* What's he want?

   B: If only he knew!

3. *A:* Want to leave a few minutes early?

   B: You don't even have to ask!

4. *A:* Isn't this a waste of time?

   B: Most of it.

5. *A:* What's her thought on this?

   B: She doesn't want to say.

Exercise 23: Sentence Completion

Complete the following sentences with information about yourself. Study the sentence before you speak so that you don't need to read it.

1. Sooner or later . . .
2. I'm sick and tired of . . .
3. One of my . . .
4. I have to have . . .
5. For once I . . .
6. Why have I . . .

*"for once" = finally

Exercise 24: Paragraph Reading

Read the following paragraph aloud. Before you begin, make sure you understand all the vocabulary. Ask your teacher or check your dictionary.

Euphemisms

A euphemism is a word or phrase that substitutes for another word or phrase to make it sound nicer. Rather than referring to someone as having died, we say he or she has "passed away." An old person is "elderly" or a "senior citizen." Sometimes though, euphemisms may seem a little ridiculous. In California, some car washers call themselves "vehicle appearance specialists," while used cars are "previously owned." Janitors are known as "sanitary engineers." Rather than going on a diet, people try "nutritional avoidance therapy." And hospitals refer to death as a "negative patient outcome"!

Exercise 25: Short Presentation

Study the following information. Using your own words, put together a short, one-minute talk describing the kinds of academic degrees available in North America. You can refer to your notes but don't read them as you speak. Your teacher will choose one aspect (part) of pronunciation for you to focus on.

Undergraduate and Graduate Degrees

The following degrees are available from most four-year colleges or universities:

B.A.: Bachelor of Arts/B.S.: Bachelor of Science

Bachelor degrees are earned after completing the freshman, sophomore, junior, and senior years of college (usually 4 years if you go straight through).

M.A.: Master of Arts/M.S.: Master of Science

Master's degrees are graduate degrees, awarded after a bachelor's degree, and usually take 2–3 additional years of study.

Ph.D.: Doctor of Philosophy (Doctorate)

A doctorate usually takes two to several more years of study after the master's. It requires a thesis in which the individual must contribute something new to the field of study.

Exercise 26: Picture Description

Say as much as you can about the picture in one minute.

8

Sentence Rhythm

Part I: Sentence Stress and Unstress

(a) succeed

(b) We skiied.

(c) advantage

(d) It shocked them.

(e) closeness

(f) Do it.

You know from Chapter 1 that when an English word with more than one syllable is pronounced, the syllables in the word are NOT equal in length or strength. One syllable is longer and stronger, and the other syllables are shorter and weaker, as in (a), (c), and (e).

Similarly, in phrases and sentences, there are usually longer, stronger words and shorter, weaker words, as in (b), (d), and (f). This pattern of strong and weak gives English its rhythm.

Native speakers expect the most important words to be emphasized. As you have learned, if you stress the wrong syllable, your speech will be very difficult to understand. Similarly, if you stress the wrong word, or if you make the syllables and words the same length and loudness, your speech will again be very difficult to understand.

Exercise 1: Listening and Production

Part A: Listen to the following sets of single words and words in groups. Each set has the same number of syllables and the same pattern of stronger and weaker syllables. Write the number of syllables and mark the long and short syllables over them.

Single Word	Words in Group	No. of Syllables
1. succeed	He left.	_____
2. dangerous	Talk to her.	_____
3. umbrella	a red one	_____
4. modernization	We should have bought it.	_____
5. impossible	the four of them	_____

Check your answers.

6. characteristic	some of that paper	_____
7. guarantee	What's your name?	_____
8. downtown	Go home.	_____
9. education	under pressure	_____
10. Japanese	Have some tea.	_____

Part B: Practice saying these words and word groups. Make the stressed syllables really long.

Exercise 2: Listening

Listen to the following pairs of phrases or sentences. Each pair has the same number of syllables.

If they have the same **stress** pattern, write **S**. If they have different stress patterns, write **D**.

1. __S__ I'm leaving you.

       He's eaten some.

2. _____ John does.

       She slept.

3. _____ Open it.

    Take it out.

4. _____ their education

    He has a problem.

5. _____ with his friend

    a report

6. _____ Promise me again.

    This must be the one.

Exercise 3: Listening

Listen to the phrases again. Underline the **strongest** syllable in each group of words. Listen once more and **decide** how many syllables each pair has. Tap the rhythm with your **finger** or a pencil as you listen.

No. of Syllables

1. __4__ I'm <u>lea</u>ving you.

    He's <u>ea</u>ten some.

2. _____ John does.

    She slept.

3. _____ Open it.

    Take it out.

4. _____ their education

    He has a problem.

5. _____ with his friend

    a report

6. _____ Promise me again.

    This must be the one.

Exercise 4: Listening

If the following pairs of words have the same **stress** pattern, write **S**. If they have different stress patterns, write **D**. (Each pair will have the same number of syllables.)

1. _____ from the beginning

    over the mountains

2. _____ They talked about it.

    All of us escaped.

3. _____ He and I were recorded.

    I didn't know the answer.

4. _____ She listened quietly.

    The man was unhappy.

5. _____ I don't know why.

    He isn't here.

6. _____ They gave him theirs.

    Sue's coat is green.

Exercise 5: Listening

Listen to the phrases again. Underline the strongest syllable in each group of words. Listen once more and decide how many syllables each pair has. Tap the rhythm with your finger or a pencil as you listen.

No. of Syllables

1. _____ from the beginning

    over the mountains

2. _____ They talked about it.

    All of us escaped.

3. _____ He and I were recorded.

    I didn't know the answer.

4. _____ She listened quietly.

   The man was unhappy.

5. _____ I don't know why.

   He isn't here.

6. _____ They gave him theirs.

   Sue's coat is green.

Part II: Content and Function Words

Words that are usually stressed more strongly are called **content** words. They include the following:

nouns: John, hunger

verbs: eaten, know

adjectives: unhappy, green

adverbs: out, quietly, again

demonstrative pronouns: this, these

possessive pronouns: theirs, ours

reflexive pronouns: myself,

   themselves

interrogative pronouns: what, why

The words in a sentence that are usually shorter and weaker are called **function** words. They include the following:

auxiliary verbs: do, have, be (when

   not the main verb)

prepositions: in, about, of

conjunctions: and, but,

determiners: a, an, the, some

personal pronouns: I, he, it,

possessive adjectives: my, your, our

Look back at the words in Exercises 3 and 5. As you think about the grammar, you will see that the content words receive the stress and the function words are weaker.

Exercise 6: Listening

Listen to the following sentences. Remember that when a content word with more than one syllable is in a sentence, it is stressed on the same syllable that is stressed when it is pronounced alone.

Example: sucCEED; He WANTS to sucCEED.

1. Was the TEST EAsy or DIfficult?
2. I'd LIKE a CUP of COffee and a croiSSANT, PLEASE.
3. She's LIStened to the TAPE Often.
4. WHEN are you PLAnning to TRAvel?
5. They were HAppy to GIVE it to us.
6. The LAKE was FROzen SOlid.
7. I DID it mySELF, with NO HELP from my TEAcher.
8. Your TIcket is HERE in your BRIEFcase.

Exercise 7: Listening

Fill in the blanks with the words you hear. (They will be content words.) Notice that because they are stressed, they are easier to hear.

1. The _____ hit her _____ on the _____.

2. _____ are you _____ to _____?

3. This _____ has _____ _____ in it.

4. You can _____ in the _____ bed.

5. _____ one isn't _____.

6. I've _____ _____ it.

7. _____ was your _____ here?

8. She _____ to stop _____ so _____.

Exercise 8: Production

Fill in the blanks with the content words of your choice. They should fit the grammar of the sentence. (They can be a little crazy, e.g., "The WOMAN hit her UMBRELLA on the HAMBURGER.") Dictate your sentences to a partner. Be sure to stress the content words when you read them.

1. The _____ hit her _____ on the _____.

2. _____ are you _____ to _____?

3. This _____ has _____ _____ in it.

4. You can _____ in the _____ bed.

5. _____ one isn't _____.

6. I've _____ _____ it.

7. _____ was _____ _____ here?

8. She _____ to stop _____ so _____.

Exercise 9: Listening and Production

Underline the content words and their stressed syllable. Then listen to see if you have underlined correctly. Mark a (/) where the speaker pauses. Finally, read it aloud, stressing and pausing where appropriate.

> Give me the peace to accept the things I can't change,
>
> give me the courage to change the things I can, and the
>
> knowledge to know the difference.*

Exercise 10: Listening and Production

Part A: Read the following dialogue. Underline the content words. Then listen to the dialogue. Notice that the content words are stressed.

A: What's the matter?

B: I lost my glasses.

A: Do you have any idea where you left them?

B: Sort of. They're around here somewhere.

A: Why don't you look for them?

B: I can't see without my glasses on!

Part B: Practice pronouncing this dialogue.

*A simplified version of a well-known poem

Exercise 11: Listening and Production

Part A: Read the following riddles to yourself. (Riddles are a popular kind of joke or puzzle in many cultures.) Check vocabulary or meaning that you don't understand with your teacher. Listen as these riddles are read aloud. Then, practice reading them with a partner. Be sure to stress the content words.

1. What is gray, has four legs, and a trunk?
   Answer: A mouse going on vacation.
2. What two things can you never have for breakfast?
   Answer: Lunch and dinner.
3. What time is it when the clock strikes thirteen?
   Answer: Time to get the clock fixed.
4. Which hand do you stir your coffee or tea with?
   Answer: Neither. I use a spoon.
5. What did the ceiling say to the wall?
   Answer: Meet me at the corner.
6. What do you call a person who doesn't have all his or her fingers on one hand?
   Answer: Normal. Fingers are supposed to be on two hands.

What is gray, has four legs, and a trunk?

7. A farmer is served two freshly laid **eggs** for breakfast each morning. But, he doesn't own any **chickens**; he doesn't beg, buy, or steal the eggs from anyone. He doesn't trade for them or find them, and they are not given to him. Where do the eggs come from?

   Answer: His ducks.

Part B: Read these riddles to a native **speaker** or another student who hasn't heard them. See if he or she **can guess** the answers. (Remember to stress the content words.)

Exercise 12: Listening and Production

Part A: Underline the content words (stressed **syllable** if a word has more than one syllable).

1. Show me the picture on your passport **or driver's** license. What do you think of it?

2. What was one of the most difficult **tests** you **have** ever taken? Tell me about it.

3. If you were granted a wish, what would it be?

4. What foreign countries have you visited?

   What foreign languages have you studied?

   What languages would you like to learn in the future?

5. Tell me about a favorite place, **somewhere** that you enjoyed a lot. Where is it? When were you there? Who were you with or who did you meet?

6. What places would you especially like to visit in the world that you haven't seen yet?

Part B: Listen as these sentences are pronounced. Check your answers. With a partner, practice pronouncing them. When you are comfortable with them, take turns asking **and** answering them. Have a real conversation, but don't forget to stress the content words and to make the function words **much** shorter than the content words.

Part III: Stress Timing

(a) KIDS LIKE DOGS.

(b) The KIDS LIKE DOGS.

(c) The KIDS LIKE the DOGS.

(d) The KIDS might LIKE the DOGS.

(e) The KIDS might have LIKED the DOGS.

(f) CATS CHASE MICE.

(g) The CATS CHASE MICE.

(h) The CATS CHASE the MICE.

(i) The CATS have CHASED the MICE.

(j) The CATS didn't CHASE the MICE.

English is a **stress-timed*** language. This means that speakers try to make the STRESSED syllables come at equal spaces. It also means that if there are three or four unstressed syllables between the stressed syllables, they will be pronounced faster and reduced more so that the speaker can reach the next "beat" on time.

Also, if two stressed syllables are not separated by any unstressed syllables, they will often be stretched out longer in order to space them equally.

The time it takes to say a sentence in English depends on the number of stressed syllables, not on the total number of syllables. **Unstressed syllables do not count**.

*In contrast, many languages are syllable-timed. In such languages, the more syllables a sentence has, the more time it will take to say. Also, the syllables are basically equal in length, giving these languages a very even rhythm. If you speak English with every syllable equally stressed, your English will have a very un-English rhythm, and this will make it more difficult to understand.

Exercise 13: Listening and Production*

Listen to the following sentences and phrases, and then practice pronouncing them. Each group has the same number of STRESSED syllables, although the number of unstressed syllables is different. Because the stressed syllables count in the timing, they take the same amount of time to say. As unstressed syllables are added, they have to be squeezed in so that the regular beat of the stressed syllables is not delayed. Try to keep the stressed syllables evenly spaced apart. Tap your pencil on the table to help you keep the timing.

*Adapted from the *Manual of American English Pronunciation*, 4th ed.

1. a) The DANES   BROUGHT   BREAD and CHEESE.

   b) The CaNAdians are ORdering some HAMburgers and COffee.

Note: To squeeze in the unstressed syllables, you need to relax the face muscles and to reduce the unstressed vowels to /ə/. At the same time, you need to move the tongue quickly through the consonants of the unstressed syllables. The mouth and jaw open for stressed syllables and their vowels only, and then close and relax again for the unstressed syllables.

Four Stressed Syllables				Actual Syllables
2. a) ONE	TWO	THREE	FOUR	4
b) FIVE	SIX	SEven	EIGHT	5
c) NINE	TEN	eLEven	TWELVE	6
d) THIRteen	FOURteen	FIFteen	SIXteen	8
e) SEventeen	EIGHteen	NINEteen	TWENty	9

Three Stressed Syllables	Actual Syllables
3. a. Sith is Thai.	3
b. Paul is French.	3
c. Hans is German.	4
d. David is Czech.	4
e. Hilal is Turkish.	5
f. Lisa is Swedish.	5
g. Fanny is Chinese.	5
h. Chuck-he is Korean.	6
i. Cynthia is Mexican.	7
j. Hendra is Indonesian.	7
k. Abdullah is Kuwaiti.	7
l. Hiroyuki is Japanese.	8
m. Jedediah is Canadian.	9

| | | | Four Stressed Syllables | | | | Actual Syllables |
| | | | | | | | |

Four Stressed Syllables							Actual Syllables
4. JANE	GOT		THERE	LATE.			4
PAtrick	had	LEFT	by	THREE		o'CLOCK.	8
NaOmi	will	aRRIVE	before	SCHOOL	has	STARted.	12

Now you decide where the stress falls.

Nathaniel will have finished it by the end of the month.   14

_____.   14

The Macnamaras may have adopted him by the beginning of November.   19

_____.   19

Remember: "squeezing" the unstressed syllables in does not take force; rather, it takes *r e l a x a t i o n.*

Exercise 14: Listening and Production

Listen to this famous children's rhyme. Underline the stressed words or syllables. Notice how the strong rhythmic beats fall naturally on the content words. Then read it aloud, and make a wish!

Star light, star bright

First star I see tonight.

I wish I may, I wish I might

Have this wish I wish tonight: _____

Exercise 15: Listening and Production

Listen to the following sentences. Notice that as each new phrase is added, the stressed syllables remain equally spaced. Practice pronouncing them. Tap your pencil on the table to help you keep the timing.

1. a. He told you.
    b. He told you already.
    c. He told you already that he'd pay you.
    d. He told you already that he'd pay you the money.
    e. He told you already that he'd pay you the money he bor-
       rowed.
    f. He told you already that he'd pay you the money he bor-
       rowed at the restaurant.
    g. He told you already that he'd pay you the money he bor-
       rowed at the restaurant last weekend.
    h. He told you already that he'd pay you the money he bor-
       rowed at the restaurant last weekend. Okay?

2. a. I found the tape.
    b. I found the tape that you wanted.
    c. I found the tape that you wanted to hear.
    d. I found the tape that you wanted to hear on the shelf.
    e. I found the tape that you wanted to hear on the shelf beside
       the telephone.
    f. I found the tape that you wanted to hear on the shelf beside
       the telephone in the kitchen.
    g. I found the tape that you wanted to hear on the shelf beside
       the telephone in the kitchen under some newspapers.
    h. I found the tape that you wanted to hear on the shelf beside
       the telephone in the kitchen under some newspapers that
       had buried it.

Note: The correct rhythm and stress timing is very difficult to learn
and will take a lot of practice and time. Don't give up if you can't
do it after a few days. It is very important that you practice every
day. Many language researchers believe that incorrect rhythm gives
a nonnative speaker much more of an accent than incorrectly pronouncing vowels and consonants.

CHAPTER REVIEW

Exercise 16: Paragraph Reading

Read the following paragraph aloud. Before you begin, make sure
you understand all the vocabulary. Ask your teacher or check your
dictionary. Focus on the sentence rhythm and linking.

Sales Tax

In North America, a sales tax is usually added to the
price of an item. The price you pay is almost never what
the sticker or tag says! The tax can range from about
4% to 8% and varies from place to place. For example,
the tax in one area may be 7.8% but in another, only 15
minutes away, 8.0%. In some places, food items are
taxed, but in others, they are not. In the United States,
a few states have no sales tax, but people must pay a
state income tax in addition to the federal income tax
that everyone must pay.

Exercise 17: Short Presentation

Study the following information. Using your own words, put together a short, one-minute talk about tipping customs in the U.S.
You can refer to your notes but don't read them as you speak. Your
teacher will choose one aspect (part) of pronunciation for you to
focus on.

Tipping in North America

If you are pleased with the service, here are some guide-
lines for tipping:

Restaurants: 10–20% of the total bill, including tax.
                15% is about average.

Leave a tip at restaurants where the food is brought to
you. Don't tip at fast food establishments! In some
places, e.g., expresso bars, you may see a cup on the
counter with the word "tips" on it. If you'd like, you can
leave a tip.

Taxis: 10–20%

Porters at airports, bellhops at hotels: average is about
$1 per suitcase.

Haircuts (a more recent custom): $1 to $5 depending
on how extensive the service is.

Exercise 18: Picture Description

Say as much as you can about the picture in one minute.

9

Information Focus and Intonation

Part I: Information Focus: The Basic Pattern

(a) **Sue went** to the **store**.

(b) **Long time**, **no see**.

(c) **What** can I **do** for you?

(d) My **sister threw** it to me.

(e) I **think** you should **try** it.

(f) Has her **room**mate **thought** about it?

(g) Would you **write** my **name** in Korean for me?

In Chapter 8, you learned that **content words** (nouns, main verbs, etc.) are usually stressed, and that **function words** (auxiliary verbs, prepositions, etc.) are not usually stressed.

However, the content words in a sentence are NOT stressed equally. There is always one content word that receives more stress (emphasis) than the others. You will notice the voice goes up on this word. This most-emphasized content word is sometimes called the INFORMATION FOCUS.

Often, when just one sentence is said, or when a conversation or topic is just beginning, the information focus is the LAST content word in the sentence. You will notice that the pitch or tune in the sentence is higher at the information focus.

Note: Some languages use word order to show emphasis. But in English, the speaker shows the listener what to pay more attention to by changing the pitch or tune of the sentence on the information focus word. The speaker's voice will go up noticeably on that word (or stressed syllable if it has more than one syllable). Then it will go down or continue to go up a little, depending on the sentence type. The speaker will usually have only one information focus (rise in pitch) for each short sentence, clause, or phrase. This is because emphasizing too many words is confusing to the listener.

Exercise 1: Listening

Listen to the following sentences. Notice the strong rise in pitch on the information focus (marked with a •).

1. I'd **ra**ther **not** dis**cuss** it.

I'd rather not discuss it.

2. **What kind** of **car** are you **loo**king for?
3. **How** are you **do**ing?
4. **This job** is **just** the be**gi**nning!
5. **Why** didn't you **call**?
6. Should I **o**ffer to **pay** him?
7. Is there **some**thing I can **help** you with?
8. Do you **think** I can **do** it?
9. You didn't turn **off** the **o**ven?
10. He's **got** the **flu**?

You learned in Part I of this chapter that where the pitch jumps the most from one word to another is the most important word in a group. In English, this higher pitch is part of the rising and falling patterns of speech. This melody across groups of words is called **intonation**.

Part II: Common Intonation Patterns

There are basic patterns for English intonation. These patterns have four common pitch levels:

2	**normal**	(where the voice most often is)
3	**high**	(where the voice usually rises to at the intonation focus)
1	**low**	(where the voice falls to at the end of most types of sentences)
4	**very high**	(the voice rises to show stronger emotions such as surprise, disbelief, fear, excitement)

You will see however, that the most **basic** patterns use just three. (The fourth is reserved for stronger emotions.)

Here are some of the more commonly used intonation patterns in English:

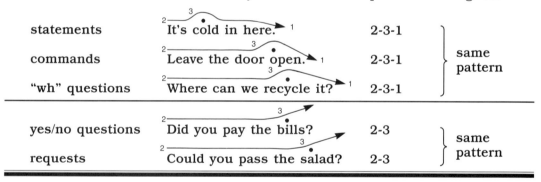

statements	It's cold in here.	2-3-1
commands	Leave the door open.	2-3-1
"wh" questions	Where can we recycle it?	2-3-1

same pattern

yes/no questions	Did you pay the bills?	2-3
requests	Could you pass the salad?	2-3

same pattern

How High or Low Should Intonation Go? How high or low the voice goes varies from speaker to speaker. It can depend on how high or low a voice the speaker has, and how expressive the speaker wants to be. Learning intonation is not like learning a song because there are no exact sets of notes to learn.

Note: The low pitch is quite low. It is at the very bottom of the speaker's voice. If the voice doesn't drop far enough, the listener will feel you are not finished and will expect you to say more. This can cause uncomfortable silences as the listener waits for you to finish your turn, or can make the listener feel that you are unsure about what you're saying.

As mentioned earlier, using level 4 pitch, or a wider range, indicates stronger emotion. On the other hand, using a very narrow range, or flat intonation, tends to signal lack of interest or boredom to the native speaker/listener.

Exercise 2: Listening and Production

Part A: Listen to the following sentences. The information focus for each is marked with a (•). Notice how the intonation rises from normal to high pitch at that syllable and then falls quickly to normal and then low pitch by the end of the sentence.

Statements

1. I can't drink coffee.
2. She's studying Japanese.
3. His mother's an architect.
4. The train's late.
5. This toothache's killing me.

Commands

6. Be careful.
7. Just don't think about it.
8. Tell me the truth.
9. Now, write a brief summary for me.
10. Stop it.

Wh-Questions

11. Why were you so angry?
12. When can we get together for lunch?
13. How can I help you?
14. What part of the city does he live in?
15. How much do those tires cost?

Part B: Practice saying these sentences by repeating after your teacher, or by talking over the voice on the tape, or by taking turns listening and speaking with a partner.

Intonation Tip: If you are not sure about your intonation, or you want more practice, find a tape of a native speaker's voice that you like and talk *over* (on top of) it, rather than repeating after it. Listen to see if your voice is going up and down the same amount and in the same places as the voice on the tape.

Exercise 3: Production

Read the following wh-questions and write your own short answers for each of them. Decide where the information focus for your answers should be and mark each with a (•). Then, with a partner, take turns asking the questions and answering them.

1. What would you líke?   I'd like _____

2. Who's thát?   That's _____

3. Why were you láte?   Because _____

4. What did you forgét?   I _____

5. Where are you góing?   To _____

Optional Practice.   In small groups or with the class, one student asks a wh-question and designates another student to answer it. Then that student asks the same or a different question of another student, and so on, until everyone has had a chance to ask and answer at least once.

Exercise 4: Production

Same as before.

1. What tíme is it?   It's _____

2. How are you féeling?   I'm _____

3. Where were you bórn?   In _____

4. When did you finally get úp?   At _____

5. What's your favorite fóod?   _____

Exercise 5: Listening and Production

Part A: Listen to the following sentences. The information focus for each is marked with a (•). Notice how the intonation rises from normal to high pitch at that syllable and stays up or goes a little higher until the end of the sentence.

Yes/no questions ⟶

1. Has he fínished it?

2. Do I have to mémorize all this?

3. Can you cóme?

4. Is this going to be on the tést?

5. And this is your bróther?

Requests ⟶

6. Would you shut the wíndow?

7. Could you lend me a dóllar?

8. Can you help him carry those bóxes?

9. Would you please explain this wórd?

10. Could I borrow some súgar?

Part B: Practice saying these sentences by repeating after your teacher, or by talking over the voice on the tape, or by taking turns listening and speaking with a partner.

Exercise 6: Dialogue Practice

Practice the following dialogues with a partner. Before you read your sentence, study it for a moment so that when you speak, you can look at your partner without reading. Mark the information focus and pay particular attention to the intonation.

1. *A:* I heard you got engaged.

   B: Yeah. Last weekend. Who told you?

   A: Someone at work. News travels quickly.

   B: I'll say.

2. *A:* Is this seat taken?

   B: No. You're welcome to sit here.

3. *A:* This place's a mess.

   B: You said it!*

*Idiom = "I really agree."

4. *A:* I'm sorry I didn't get back to you before today.

   B: I was wondering what happened.

   A: I needed to have some emergency dental work.

   B: Oh. That's too bad. Are you O.K.?

   A: I'm just glad it's over.

5. *A:* Are you still using a typewriter?

   I thought everyone used computers.

   B: Nope. This may sound crazy but I actually like to see the

   words on paper, not on a screen.

Exercise 7: Interview

Part A: Interview two native speakers of English. Write their answers in the blanks. When asking your questions, focus on the intonation for "yes/no" and "wh" questions. Try not to read them as
you speak. You may want to practice with a partner first.

1. Where were you born?
2. How do you like this city?
3. What parts of the city do you recommend for a visitor?
4. Have you ever been a student in another country?
5. What advice do you have for someone who wants to learn
   English?
6. Do you speak other languages? (Which ones?)
7. Is my English O.K.?
8. How would you recommend someone improve their English?

Answers:

1.	1.
2.	2.
3.	3.
4.	4.
5.	5.
6.	6.

7.

8.

<hr>
(signature)

7.

8.

<hr>
(signature)

Part B: Report your answers to the class or small group your teacher assigns.

Part III: *Contrasting New Information*

(a) She **ate** some **beans**.	REVIEW
(b) The **pa**per was **cut** into **lit**tle **pie**ces.	—Content words are stressed. —Function words are unstressed.
(c) I'll **see** you **next Fri**day. (d) **Say** he**llo** to your **wife** for us. (e) **When** can I **talk** to you about it?	—The most important content word gets the most stress. This word is often the LAST content word (see Part I).

(f) *A:* I **found** my **key**.
   B: **Which** key?
   A: My **house key**.
   B: Are you **sure** it's not **my** house key?
   A: **Sure am**. Here's **your house key**. You **dropped** it out**side** this **mor**ning.
	However, the speaker can break the above rules and emphasize **any** word, even if it isn't the last content word. It can even be a function word. We do this to emphasize NEW information, to CONTRAST a word with another, or to give SPECIAL MEANING to a word.

Exercise 8: Listening

Listen for the information focus in each sentence (marked with a •). Notice how the speaker emphasizes the important new ideas.

Dialogue I

A: I'm **looking** for a **car**.

B: **What type** of **car**? ("Car" is now old information. "Type" is the new information.)

A: A **used car**.

B: **Any used car**?

A: **No**, an **almost-new** car, but **not** at a **new price**.

Dialogue II

A: **Whose dog**?

B: **My dog**.

A: **Your dog**! I didn't **know** you **had** a **dog**.

B: I **didn't have** a dog. She's **new**.

A: **New**? **How new**?

B: **Brand new**. I **just got** her **ye**sterday.

Exercise 9: Listening and Production

First, listen and underline the information focus (new or contrasting idea) in each sentence. Then, with a partner, practice saying these dialogues, emphasizing the underlined words (or syllables).

Dialogue I

A: Hi. How are you doing?

B: Fine. How are you doing?

A: Pretty good.
My name's Jim. What's yours?

B: Jane. I'm not from here. I'm from Oregon. What about you?

A: California.

For additional practice, substitute your own names.

Dialogue II

A: I have to buy a book.

B: What kind of book?

A: A textbook.

B: For grammar or for reading?

A: I have those books already. This one's for pronunciation.

Exercise 10: Listening

Listen as the information focus changes to show which idea in the sentence the speaker wants to emphasize.

	Meaning
1. Can I borrow this book for a **WEEK**?	(Or is a week too long?)
2. Can I borrow this **BOOK** for a week?	(not something else)
3. Can I borrow **THIS** book for a week?	(this book, not a different one)
4. Can I **BORROW** this book for a week?	(I'm only borrowing it, not taking it)
5. Can **I** borrow this book for a week?	(Do you trust me, in contrast to someone else?)
6. **CAN** I borrow this book for a week?	(Can I or can't I? Make up your mind.)

Exercise 11: Production

Decide which word in each sentence needs to be emphasized to give the meaning in the parentheses and underline it. Then practice pronouncing each sentence, making your voice go up on the emphasized word.

	Meaning
1. Did you leave the money on your desk?	(and not in your wallet or pocket)
2. Did you leave the money on your desk?	(and not on someone else's desk)
3. Did you leave the money on your desk?	(and not in it)
4. Did you leave the money on your desk?	(rather than take it with you)
5. Did you leave the money on your desk?	(or did someone else leave it)
6. Did you leave the money on your desk?	(I'm not clear—did you, or didn't you do this)

7. Did you leave the money on your desk?   (I know people leave pencils and paper on their desks, but I'm surprised you'd leave money there.)

Exercise 12: Production

Pronounce the following sentence in different ways in order to answer each question that follows:

That is my new black leather jacket.

1. What's that?
2. Whose new jacket is that?
3. Is that your new jacket, or your old one?
4. Is that his new jacket?
5. Which is your new black leather jacket?

Part IV: Intonation Patterns That Change the Meaning

	Intonation can change the meaning of sentences. Study the following examples:
(a) She's a doctor.	(a) a statement of fact
(b) She's a doctor?	(b) echo question, or statement of surprise or disbelief
(c) Do you want cheesecake or pie?	(c) speaker asking if the person wants dessert
(d) Do you want cheesecake or pie?	(d) speaker offering a choice
(e) Bill has eaten, hasn't he?	(e) speaker is unsure
(f) Bill has eaten, hasn't he?	(f) speaker expects agreement
(g) This could hurt Joe.	(g) talking about Joe
(h) This could hurt, Joe.	(h) talking to Joe

The following exercises will give you practice with each of these patterns.

Exercise 13: Production

Part A: Put a dot over the information focus in each sentence. Then practice saying each one, first as a statement, and then as a question, or if you like, as a statement of surprise or disbelief. (For the latter, you will need to take it to pitch level 4.)

    Example: He left.   He left?

1. The hike starts at 6:00 A.M.

2. My check bounced

3. This is what you wanted

4. There's a mid-term next week

5. We're finally finished with this

6. My fever's 102°

7. We have to take a taxi

8. Class has been cancelled

Part B: Work with a partner. One person reads each sentence, either as a statement or as a question. The other listens and says "Oh" or "O.K." if it is a statement. If a question, the response is "That's right."

Choice Questions

A choice question is a question with "or" in it. There are two common intonation patterns for choice questions. They each have different meanings and each needs a different kind of answer.

The first pattern (a) is called **open choice**—a kind of yes/no question. It is called open because there are choices.

The second pattern (b) is called **closed choice** because the speaker is offering a limited choice. An answer of "yes" or "no" would be strange.

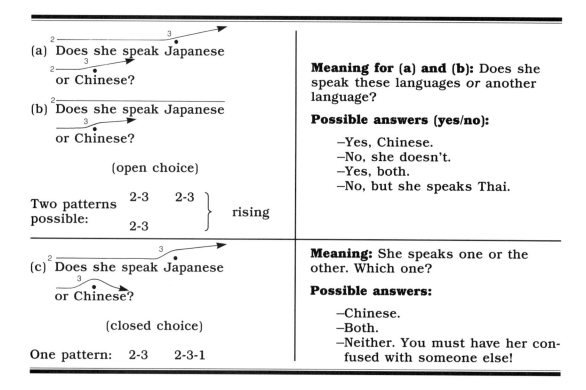

Exercise 14: Listening and Production

Part A: Listen to the following short conversations. The first five have **open choice** questions, and the second five have **closed choice** questions. Notice the answers.

Open Choice

1. *A:* Do you take cream or sugar?

   B: Neither. I like it black.

2. *A:* Can I bring a salad or dessert or some wine?

   B: Sure, whichever is easiest for you.

3. *A:* Would you like to play cards or Scrabble?

   B: O.K. But let me finish reading this chapter first.

4. *A:* Does he sing or play an instrument?

 B: Yes, he's really talented. He has a great voice, plays classical guitar, and he's a good dancer, too.

5. *A:* Have you ever been to Europe or the Middle East?

 B: No, but I was in South America once.

Closed Choice

6. *A:* Should I get tickets for gymnastics or basketball?

 B: Gymnastics is my preference. I love the floor exercises.

7. *A:* Which kind of music do you prefer: rock or classical?

 B: It depends. I like both.

8. *A:* What do you want for breakfast, eggs or cereal?

 B: Neither. I'm not hungry. Just decaf will do me fine.

9. *A:* Could you hand me a screwdriver?

 B: This one or that one?

 A: That one on the floor.

10. *A:* Were you closer to your mother or your father?

 B: My mother. My father wasn't home much.

Part B: Practice these conversations. Work in groups of three: two speakers and one listener. The listener should watch for correct information focus and intonation.

Exercise 15: Listening and Production

Part A: Listen as each question is asked. Draw arrows to show the intonation you hear. Choose the most appropriate response for each. Check your answers. Then, practice reading each question and response with a partner.

1. Would you like coffee or tea?

   (a.) Coffee, please.

   b. Yes, I'd love some coffee.

2. Would you enjoy seeing a movie or a play?

   a. Maybe. How about a concert?

   b. A play sounds nice.

3. Did she buy some oranges or bananas?

   a. No, she ran out of money.

   b. Bananas. She knows I hate oranges.

4. Shall we play Poker or Hearts?

   a. Poker sounds good.

   b. No, I'm too tired.

5. Should I wear black or navy blue?

   a. No, they're both dark.

   b. You look better in black.

Part B: Look at the five answers that were not circled. Make an appropriate question for those using the same words but different intonation. Practice the questions and responses with a partner.

Tag Questions

A **tag question** is a statement followed by a short yes/no question (called a "tag"), so each part has its own information focus. There are two common patterns:

(a) **You're hungry, aren't you?**	(I'm not sure if you're hungry.)
(b) **You're hungry, aren't you?**	(I expect you to answer "yes.")

When the intonation on the tag goes up, the speaker is unsure. If the intonation goes down, the speaker is sure.

Exercise 16: Listening and Production

Part A: Listen to the following sentences as they are pronounced with the two different patterns. Note the different meanings.

1. a. It isn't going to snow, is it?   (unsure)

    b. It isn't going to snow, is it?   (sure)

2. a. She hasn't left yet, has she?   (unsure)

    b. She hasn't left yet, has she?   (sure)

3. a. You'll tell them, won't you?   (unsure)

    b. You'll tell them, won't you?   (sure)

4. a. She can do it, can't she?   (unsure)

    b. She can do it, can't she?   (sure)

5. a. They'll visit us, won't they?   (unsure)

    b. They'll visit us, won't they?   (sure)

Part B: Work with a partner. One partner says either sentence (a) or (b). If pattern (a) is heard, the listener says, "You sound unsure." If pattern (b) is heard, the response is "You sound sure."

Talking To (Direct Address)

(a) Mr. Thompson, it's been decided.	When addressing (talking to) another person and using a name or title, rising intonation is usually used.
(b) It's been decided, Mr. Thompson.	
(c) Mark, are you okay?	Notice that the name has its own information focus and intonation contour.
(d) Are you okay, Mark?	
(e) Why are you late again, Douglas? (annoyed)	If your voice stays flat, the listener may think you are annoyed or angry, as in (e).

Exercise 17: Listening and Production

Part A: Listen to the following groups of sentences with direct address.

(pattern) name first: 2–3   2–3–1

1. Sandy, I'd like you to meet Doug.
2. Patricia, let's go for a walk.
3. Bob, don't wait for me.
4. Officer, I wasn't speeding, was I?

(pattern) name last: 2–3–1   2–3

5. How's your garden doing, Kim?
6. Excuse me, Miss.
7. I'm done with the phone, Jim.
8. Hi, guys!

Part B: Practice pronouncing these sentences.

Exercise 18: Production

In groups of 3–5 students, form a circle. Make sure everyone knows and can pronounce everyone else's names. (Use name tags if necessary.) Then, take turns going around the circle, doing the following:

1. Address the person on your left and ask him or her a wh-question. That person will answer your question. (Group members not speaking can monitor and offer suggestions.)

   Example: A: _____, what other classes are you
                          (name)
           taking now?

           B: Response

2. Address the person on your right and ask him or her a yes/no question. That person will answer your question. Other group members monitor.

   Example: A: Do you like popcorn, _____?
                                (name)

           B: I love it!

3. Address any person in your group. Give him or her a compliment (say something nice about him or her). That person will respond, "Thank you, _____."

Example: A: I really like those boots, _____.
                                               (name)

                B: Thank you, _____,
                                    (name)

4. Address any person in your group. Make a request. That person can respond however he or she wants to.

Example: A: _____, would you like to do my home-
                     (name)
                work for me?

                B: No way! I've got enough homework of my own,

                    _____.
                        (name)

5. Address a person in your group and ask a tag question. That person will respond.

Example: A: Nice day, isn't it, _____?
                                       (name)

                B: I'll say.

Talking About

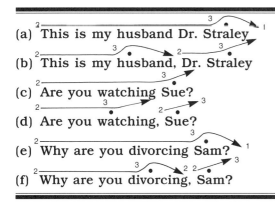

When talking about another person, the name is in the same intonation contour as the rest of the sentence. The intonation will vary depending on whether it is a statement, "wh" or yes/no question, and follow those patterns accordingly.

Remember, when you are talking TO someone, there are two intonation patterns **within** the sentence, and the intonation rises on the name.

Exercise 19: Listening

Decide if the speaker is "talking to" or "talking about" someone. Circle the letter for the sentence that has the same meaning as the sentence you hear.

1. *A.* I enjoy seeing Jack.

   B. I like seeing that.

2. *A.* Jill is going to pay for something.

   B. Jill is going to receive money.

3. *A.* I'm surprised you want to visit Bill.

   B. I'm surprised Bill can see.

4. *A.* Dr. Robb is being studied.

   B. Some people are studying.

Check your answers.

5. *A.* She made a bet.

   B. She made a bet with Sue.

6. *A.* It's difficult to judge Ms. Brown.

   B. I can't judge that very well.

7. *A.* I don't like to watch Gail.

   B. That is boring to watch.

8. *A.* Kelly needs help.

   B. Kelly is helping someone.

Exercise 20: Listening and Production

Part A: Listen to the following sentences. Note that the intonation will differ according to whether it is a statement, "wh" or yes/no question.

1. Why are you watching Sue?

2. How much are you giving Jack?

3. It's easy to like Tom.

4. How did you hear Professor James?

5. I'd like to divorce Bob.

6. It's interesting to see Mary.

7. What did you knit Kim?

8. How could you watch Terry?

Part B: Practice pronouncing these sentences. Then, insert commas and practice pronouncing them according to the correct pattern for direct address.

Part V: Lists

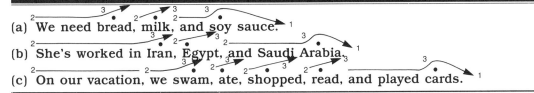

(a) We need bread, milk, and soy sauce.

(b) She's worked in Iran, Egypt, and Saudi Arabia.

(c) On our vacation, we swam, ate, shopped, read, and played cards.

The intonation pattern used to list or name a series of things, rises or stays up until the last thing on the list. Then, the voice rises and falls to show that the list is finished.

PATTERN: 2–3   2–3   2–3–1

Exercise 21: Listening and Production

Listen as the following sentences with lists are said. Then, with a partner, take turns pronouncing them.

1. We're going to Morocco, Spain, and Portugal.
2. He has black, brown, and gray shoes.
3. I need olive oil, basil, and garlic to cook this.
4. She met his mother, grandmother, and younger sister.
5. Three mountains that she would like to climb are Mt. Kilamanjaro, Mt. Fuji, and Mt. Everest.

Exercise 22: Production

Create your own lists by filling in the blanks below. Then, with a partner, read your lists and listen to your partner's lists.

1. Three colors I like are _____, _____, and

   _____.

2. You should bring _____, _____, and _____.

3. Four things that are common in my country but are not common in North America are _____, _____,

   _____ and _____.

4. The people I enjoy most are _____, _____, and

   _____.

5. For entertainment, I like to _____, to _____ and to

   _____.

Exercise 23: Paragraph Reading

Read the following paragraph aloud. Before you begin, make sure you understand all the vocabulary. Ask your teacher or check your dictionary.

Names* in the Phone Book

Many first names in English have a long and short form—some people tend to think of them as formal and informal. It's important to be aware of both when using the phone book (particularly when looking up a man's name). For example, you may meet someone at a party named "Bob Carter." Later, you decide to call him but find that there are no "Bob Carters" listed in the phone book. Why? Many people choose to have the more formal name listed. You need to be aware of both, and may find that the majority of your male acquaintances go by the longer name in the phone book. Here are some of the more common ones for you to be familiar with:

*This paragraph deals with male names. There are also short forms for female names.

Bill	William
Jim	James
Chuck	Charles
Tom	Thomas
Greg	Gregory
Joe	Joseph
Mike	Michael
Ted	Theodore
Ed	Edward
Pat	Patrick

Exercise 24: Short Presentation

Interview one or several native speakers to find out the various short forms for females' names. Put together a short, one-minute talk about the information you receive. You can refer to your notes, but don't read them when you speak. Your teacher will choose one aspect (part) of pronunciation for you to focus on.

Exercise 25: Picture Description

Say as much as you can about the picture in one minute.

10

Inflectional Endings

Part I: Past Tense (-ed)

	-ed is pronounced as /əd/ after /t/ and /d/.*
(a) I needed more. (b) I wanted help.	Please note: When pronouncing the ending, be careful to split the word *before* /d/ or /t/ so that it begins with a consonant: 　　wan/təd　nee/dəd
(c) He talked a lot.	-ed is pronounced as /t/ after voiceless sounds,† (except /t/).
(d) She studied until midnight yesterday.	-ed is pronounced as /d/ after voiced sounds,‡ (except /d/).
(e) He talked too much. (f) She studied Latin.	In connected speech, the endings may change from the above rules. If the sound is linked as in (e) and (f), you will probably not hear the ending. (Please note that linking can also occur between two consonants that are *similar* but not the same. Such consonants are often formed in similar places in the mouth, as with *t/d* or *d/l*.)

(g) He talked too much last night. (h) She studies daily.	The context or other words in the sentence (d) can be a clue to the tense. The grammar (3rd person -s) can also be helpful: compare (g) and (h).
(i) I wanted more time. (j) I needed directions.	For pronunciation purposes, it is more important that an ending *be heard*, rather than if it is exactly a /t/ or /d/. This is especially true of the /əd/ ending; make sure that at least an extra *syllable* can be heard.

*In some dialects, an /I/ is used instead of /ə/ for the *ed* ending.
†The voiceless sounds are /p/, /k/, /s/, /f/, /sh/, /ch/, /θ/. Put your hand on your throat and say these sounds. There will be no vibration. Since these sounds are voiceless, the ending will also be voiceless.
‡The voiced sounds are /b/, /g/, /z/, /v/, /zh/, /j/, /m/, /n/, /ng/, /l/, /r/, /ð/. There is vibration for these sounds. Since these sounds are voiced, the endings will also be voiced.

Exercise 1: Listening

Listen to the following sentences. Circle the verb you hear.

1. play   played
2. study   studied
3. fill   filled
4. misplace   misplaced
5. add   added

Check your answers.

6. ask   asked
7. cry   cried
8. start   started
9. happen   happened
10. try   tried

Exercise 2: Listening and Production

Listen to the following words. Decide if the final sound is voiced or voiceless, and then practice pronouncing the appropriate ending (/t/ or /d/).

1. like	6. dress
2. wish	7. mix
3. ask	8. believe
4. play	9. enjoy
5. measure	10. listen

Check your answers.

Exercise 3: Production: the /əd/ Ending

Practice pronouncing the following phrases. Remember to split the word BEFORE the *t* or *d*.

1. needed money
2. rented an apartment
3. waited for the bus
4. added a class
5. rested after lunch
6. decided to leave
7. flooded the town
8. lasted too long

Exercise 4: Production

With a partner, take turns reading one sentence from each pair. Have your partner circle the sentence he or she thinks you have read. Check your answers.

1. *A.* We talk about it.

   B. We talked about it.

2. *A.* I believe him.

   B. I believed him.

3. *A.* They study animals.

   B. They studied animals.

4. *A.* We mix up the names.

   B. We mixed up the names.

5. *A.* They rent from their parents.

   B. They rented from their parents.

6. *A.* I wait at least an hour.

   B. I waited at least an hour.

7. *A.* I like the potato chips.

   B. I liked the potato chips.

8. *A.* I need directions.

   B. I needed directions.

I need directions.

Exercise 5: Production

Finish the sentences (keep them short). Practice pronouncing them with a partner. Mark the linking before you speak.

1. I waited . . .
2. He mixed up . . .
3. I've never liked . . .
4. We enjoyed . . .
5. It lasted . . .
6. I've decided . . .

As follow-up, you can dictate your sentences to a partner or to a group.

Exercise 6: Production (Optional)

Same as before.

1. They played . . .
2. We believed . . .
3. I haven't measured . . .
4. We've rented . . .
5. She asked . . .
6. I wanted . . .

Exercise 7: Dictation (Optional)

Choose any eight verbs from the preceding exercises. Write both the present and past tense forms. Choose one word from each pair to dictate, either to a partner or a native speaker. Compare answers when you are finished.

	Present	Past
1.		
2.		
3.		
4.		

Check your answers.

5.		
6.		
7.		
8.		

Exercise 8: Dialogue Practice

Practice reading the following dialogues with a partner. First, mark the linking and remember to focus on the endings you have studied in this section.

Before you begin each dialogue, study your sentence for a moment so that when you speak, you can look at your partner without reading.

1. *A:* This bill isn't right.

   B: They added wrong.

2. *A:* I've asked for more help.

   B: We've really needed it.

3. *A:* Is that the way your name is spelled?

   B: No. It's way off.

4. *A:* I tried to listen carefully.

   B: It's hard with something so boring.

Part II: Plural/3rd Person "s"

(a) wish*es* pag*es* /əz/	*-es* is pronounced as /əz/ after /s/, /z/, /sh/, /ch/, /j/, and /zh/.
(b) wi/shes senten/ces pa/ges cla/sses	Remember to split the word BEFORE the final consonant sound, as in (b).
(c) wan*ts* /s/ boo*ks*	*-s* is pronounced as /s/ after voiceless sounds, except /s/, /sh/, and /ch/.
(d) nee*ds* /z/ drea*ms*	*-s* is pronounced as /z/ after voiced sounds, except /z/, /zh/, and /j/. (See Chapter 4 for /s/ and /z/ production.)
	In connected speech, the endings may change from the above rules.
(e) He leaves soon.	/z/ in "leaves" (e) may sound like /s/ because it is followed by a voiceless sound.
(f) She plays so well.	In (f), /z/ becomes voiceless because it is followed by a voiceless sound.
(g) The sentences seem boring.	
(h) She wishes she were here.	In (g) and (h), the extra syllable is heard more clearly than the particular ending because of the linking with /s/ and /sh/.
	As with the /əd/ ending, it is more important that *an ending be heard*, rather than if it is exactly /s/ or /z/. It is particularly important that at least the extra *syllable* be heard for the /əz/ ending.

Exercise 9: Listening

Listen to the following words. Circle the ending you hear.

1. /s/   /z/   /əz/

2. /s/   /z/   /əz/

3. /s/   /z/   /əz/

4. /s/   /z/   /əz/

5. /s/   /z/   /əz/

Check your answers.

6. /s/   /z/   /əz/

7. /s/   /z/   /əz/

8. /s/   /z/   /əz/

9. /s/   /z/   /əz/

10. /s/   /z/   /əz/

Exercise 10: Listening and Production

Listen to the following words. Decide if the final sound is voiced or voiceless, and then practice pronouncing the appropriate ending (/s/, /z/, or /əz/).

1. wait   6. cause
2. say   7. day
3. car   8. bus
4. make   9. sentence
5. story   10. drive

Check your answers.

Exercise 11: Production

Practice pronouncing the following phrases.

1. finishes early   4. cars and buses
2. gets ready   5. happens by chance
3. drives fast   6. washes shirts

Exercise 12: Production

Same as before.

1. pages and pages
2. reads quietly
3. hours of work
4. leaves late
5. pieces of cake
6. needs support
7. sentences sound hard
8. teaches students

Exercise 13: Production

With a partner, take turns reading one sentence from each pair. Have your partner circle the sentence he or she thinks you have read. Check your answers.

1. a. The nurse went down the hall.

    b. The nurses went down the hall.

2. a. I saw your friend at the picnic.

    b. I saw your friends at the picnic.

3. a. Do you want the window open?

    b. Do you want the windows open?

4. a. His tire went flat on the freeway.

    b. His tires went flat on the freeway.

5. a. What language did they speak?

    b. What languages did they speak?

6. a. The week passed quickly.

    b. The weeks passed quickly.

7. a. She enjoyed the book a lot.

    b. She enjoyed the books a lot.

8. a. The bus came late again.

    b. The buses came late again.

Exercise 14: Production

Finish the sentences (keep them short). Practice pronouncing them with a partner. Mark the linking before you speak.

1. It says . . .

2. That makes . . .

3. The last few days . . .

4. These sentences . . .

5. This looks . . .

Exercise 15: Production (Optional)

Same as before.

1. What exercises . . .

2. Our teacher wishes . . .

3. This takes . . .

4. Those pages . . .

5. My classes . . .

Exercise 16: Dictation (Optional)

Choose eight words (nouns or verbs) with the endings /s/, /z/, and /əz/ from the preceding exercises. Dictate them to a partner or a native speaker. Compare answers when you are finished.

1.

2.

3.

4.

5.

6.

7.

8.

Exercise 17: Dialogue Practice

Practice reading the following dialogues with a partner. First, mark the linking and remember to focus on the endings you have studied in this section.

Before you begin each dialogue, study your sentence for a moment so that when you speak, you can look at your partner without reading.

1. *A:* It's time to get some new clothes.*

   B: You finally noticed!

2. *A:* This car drives really nicely.

   B: You can say that again!

3. *A:* We've got pages and pages to read.

   B: It'll be hours of work.

4. *A:* What causes your headaches?

   B: Don't know. They're migraines.

Part III: -teen/-ty

		One way to tell the difference between these two endings is from the stress. With -teen, the stress is on the second part of the word. With -ty, the first part of the word is stressed.
(a) fifteen dollars	fif TEEN	
(b) fifty dollars	FIF ty	
(c) fourteen years	four TEEN	
(d) forty years	FOR ty	

Additionally, you will find that in the **-ty** ending, the **t** is pronounced as a flap, but the **t** in **-teen** is not.

Exercise 18: Listening

Listen to the following sentences. Circle the ending you hear.

1. -ty   -teen   4. -ty   -teen

2. -ty   -teen   5. -ty   -teen

3. -ty   -teen   6. -ty   -teen

*This word is pronounced exactly like the verb "close."

Exercise 19: Listening

Same as before.

1. -ty   -teen
2. -ty   -teen
3. -ty   -teen
4. -ty   -teen
5. -ty   -teen

Exercise 20: Production

Practice pronouncing the following phrases.

1. 17 people
2. 80 will do
3. 14 dollars
4. 15 too many
5. 90 sounds

Exercise 21: Production

Finish the following sentences (keep them short). Practice pronouncing them with a partner.

1. With $40, . . .
2. In 15 years, . . .
3. When I was 18, . . .
4. If I live to be 90, . . .
5. In 30 days, . . .
6. 50 minutes . . .

Exercise 22: Dictation

Choose one number from each pair and read it aloud with the word that follows. Have a partner or native speaker circle the phrase you dictate. Check the answers when you are finished.

1. (40   14)   people   4. (15   50)   students
2. (18   80)   miles   5. (19   90)   dollars
3. (17   70)   years   6. (13   30)   tickets

CHAPTER REVIEW

Exercise 23: Dialogue Practice

Practice reading the following dialogues with a partner. First, mark the linking and where you think the sounds might change. Remember to focus on the endings you have studied in this chapter.

Before you begin each dialogue, study your sentence for a moment so that when you speak, you can look at your partner without reading.

1. *A:* Is the 4:15 bus O.K.?

   B: 4:15? I thought you said 4:50.

2. *A:* I've got pages and pages to study.

   B: Don't you wish you had started a few weeks earlier?

3. *A:* What chapters have been covered?

   B: One through three, but only the explanations, not the exercises.

4. *A:* He needs more money than he asked for.

   B: And he's asked for a lot already.

5. *A:* We sure waste time by going to these lectures.

   B: The speaker just seems to wander.

6. *A:* It says here that the classes are closed.

   B: That can't be. There are supposed to be 13 sections of that class.

Exercise 24: Paragraph Reading

Read the following paragraph aloud. Before you begin, make sure you understand all the vocabulary. Ask your teacher or check your dictionary. (Remember that the -ion ending, as in "information" or "question," is pronounced /ən/, and is **unstressed**.)

TOEFL Test Information

There are two forms of the TOEFL test: the long and the short. The long form has an additional 80 questions which are **experimental**. They are not counted in your score but used to see if they would be good questions for TOEFL exams in the future. There is no way to know while you are taking the test which questions are experimental and which are not. Following is information that shows the difference between the two forms:

Short Form

Listening	30 minutes	50 questions
Grammar*	25 minutes	40 questions
Vocabulary and Reading Comprehension	45 minutes	60 questions

Long Form

Listening	40 minutes	80 questions
Grammar	35 minutes	60 questions
Vocabulary and Reading Comprehension	65 minutes	90 questions

*Formal Name: Structure and Written Expression

Exercise 25: Short Presentation

Study the following information. Using your own words, put together a short, one-minute talk about the cartoonist Gary Larson. You can refer to your notes, but don't read them when you speak. Your teacher will choose one aspect (part) of pronunciation for you to focus on.

Gary Larson

Author of "The Far Side" cartoon

Began 1979

Originally called "Nature's Way"

First newspaper: the *Seattle Times*

While on vacation in San Francisco, dropped off samples at the *San Francisco Chronicle*

Was offered a contract

During the same period, the *Seattle Times* decided to stop running it: too many complaints

January 1, 1980 "The Far Side" appeared in the *San Francisco Chronicle*

1982 first book: *The Far Side*

Humor enjoyed by all generations

80-million readers world-wide

Cartoons often make fun of people; animals "win"

Not only carried by more than 900 newspapers, also in cards, calendars, and on mugs

Larson and comic strip took a vacation from late 1988 through 1989

Old cartoons were run as "The Classic Far Side"

Returned January 1990

Fans are happy to have him back!

THE FAR SIDE   By GARY LARSON*

Early attempts at the milkshake

Exercise 26: Picture Description

Say as much as you can about the picture in one minute.

11

Reductions in Consonant Clusters

Part I: sts/sks/th *Deletion*

(a)	costs	*cos:s**	/t/ in an **sts** cluster can be dropped, as in (a) and (b). /k/ in an **sks** cluster is often dropped in reduced speech, as in (c) and (d).
(b)	tests	*tes:s*	
(c)	asks	*as:s*	
(d)	risks	*ris:s*	
(e)	months	*munts*	In some cases, **th** can be changed or dropped. It may become a /t/ or /k/, or θ, as in (e), (f), or (g). There are not many of these words and you will practice the most common ones in this chapter.
(f)	strengths	*strengks*	
(g)	twelfths	*twelfs*	
(h)	Is there	*zere*	In rapid speech, many speakers use a /z/ for **th** when saying "Is there" for "Is that."
(i)	Is that	*zat*	

*The ":" is used here to show the lengthening of the consonant.

Exercise 1: Listening

Fill in the blanks with the words you hear.

1. You're taking way too many _____.
2. Biology is my _____.
3. How many writing _____ are left?
4. He lives with a group of _____.
5. Nine-_____ of this must be wrong.
6. The decision _____ in your hands.
7. _____ what they decided?
8. What are his _____?
9. I think my _____ broken.
10. _____ another way to do this?

Exercise 2: Listening and Production

Part A: Listen to the following words.

1. costs	6. tasks
2. tourists	7. rests
3. tests	8. requests
4. asks	9. rusts
5. tenths	10. strengths

Part B: Practice pronouncing these words with a partner.

Exercise 3: Listening and Production

Same as before.

1. forests	5. artists
2. guests	6. invests
3. disks	7. risks
4. wrists	8. masks

Exercise 4: Production

Practice pronouncing the following phrases from Exercise 1.

1. too many risks
2. weakest subject
3. writing tasks
4. group of artists
5. $\frac{9}{10}$
6. decision rests
7. Is that
8. his strengths
9. wrist's broken
10. Is there

Part II: nt Reduction

(a) center
(b) rented
(c) twenty

When **nt** occurs in a word and is followed by a vowel sound, many speakers omit the **t** and use a flapped *n* in place of the **t**.

A flapped *n* is a flap with **nasality**.

Exercise 5: Listening

Fill in the blanks with the words you hear.

1. There's only one _____ during the

   play.

2. What time is your _____ appointment?

3. The quality is more important than the

   _____.

4. The air sure feels like _____.

5. There's _____ more where that came

   from.

6. You can always _____ him.

Is there another way to do this?

Exercise 6: Listening and Production

Part A: Listen to the following words. Mark the flapped *n*.

1. county	5. enter	9. count on
2. oriental	6. identify	10. dentist/dental
3. winter	7. mental	11. quantity
4. wanted	8. plenty	12. intermission

Part B: Practice pronouncing these words with a partner.

Exercise 7: Production

Practice pronouncing the following phrases from Exercise 5.

1. one intermission
2. dental work
3. the quantity
4. feels like winter
5. plenty more
6. count on him

Exercise 8: Production

Write five sentences about risks tourists face in another country or your own country. To help you, some words are given below. Read your sentences to the class.

tourists	risks	asks
costs	identification	plenty
months	winter time	count on

1.

2.

3.

4.

5.

Part III: Assimilation

	Sometimes in English, two sounds are linked and make a new sound. This is called **assimilation.** A very common change is with /y/:
(a) *Can't you* come?	
(b) *Should you* stay?	/t/ + /y/ = /ch/
(c) *Pass your* plate.	/d/ + /y/ = /j/
(d) *Where's your* car?	/s/ + /y/ = /sh/
	/z/ + /y/ = /zh/
	Assimilation with /t/ and /d/ is more common than with /s/ and /z/.
(e) What are you thinking? *whachya*	The auxiliary verb can be dropped as in (e), (f), and (g). Note that (e) and (f) have the same pronunciation.
(f) What do you think? *whachya*	
(g) What did you think? *whaja*	

Exercise 9: Listening

Listen to the following sentences. Underline where you hear the assimilation.

1. Haven't you heard?

2. When did you get back?

3. I caught you!

4. What are you thinking about?

5. When's your date?

6. What's your best guess?

7. Use your head!

8. I thought it's what you'd want.

9. What do you need?

10. Is that what you're planning?

Exercise 10: Production

Practice pronouncing the phrases from the previous exercise.

1. haven't you
2. did you
3. caught you
4. what are you
5. when's your

6. what's your
7. use your
8. what you'd
9. what do you
10. what you're

Exercise 11: Interview

Part A: Interview a student in the class and a native speaker of English. Write their answers in the blanks, and remember to have them sign their names. Use the reductions studied in this chapter (some of the more difficult ones are given to you in parentheses). Study each question before you speak so that you do not have to read it. You may want to practice with a partner first.

1. What did you (*whajya*) do yesterday?
2. What do you (*whachya*) do every day?
3. How did you (*howja*) get your first job?
4. When's your next vacation?
5. Where did you (*whereja*) go on your last vacation?
6. What can't you do?
7. What shouldn't you do?
8. Why did you agree to this interview?

Answers:

1.   1.

2.   2.

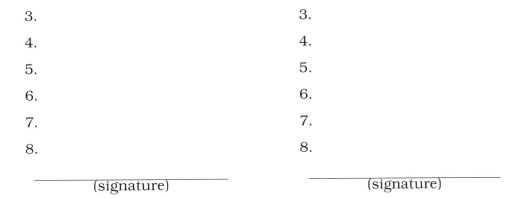

Part B: Report your answers to the class or small group your teacher assigns.

CHAPTER REVIEW

Exercise 12: Dialogue Practice

Practice pronouncing the following dialogues with a partner. Before you say your sentence, study it for a moment so that when you speak, you can look at your partner without reading. Mark the linking and where you think the sounds might change.

1. *A:* When's your last test?

    B: I don't want to think about it.

2. *A:* Need some computer disks?

    B: How did you know?

3. *A:* Isn't this what you want?

    B: I wouldn't say that.

4. *A:* The guests are here.

    B: It's about time.

5. *A:* How's your family?

    B: I haven't seen them for a few months.

6. *A:* I'm nervous about the interview.

    B: Just let them know your strengths.

Exercise 13: Sentence Completion

Complete the following sentences with an opinion you have. Study each sentence before you speak so that you don't need to read it.

1. Tourists . . .
2. School costs . . .
3. Life in this country . . .
4. Students shouldn't . . .
5. Teachers shouldn't . . .
6. Driving tests . . .
7. Dentists . . .
8. Plenty of people . . .

Exercise 14: Paragraph Reading

Read the following paragraph aloud. Before you begin, make sure you understand all the vocabulary. Ask your teacher or check your dictionary.

Test of Written English (TWE)

Four times a year the TOEFL offers the TWE, Test of Written English. This is a 30-minute essay exam. There are two types of questions on the exam. The first is to compare and contrast an issue and argue about it, and the second is to describe and discuss a graph or chart. The test is read and scored by two readers. The lowest score is a "1," which means "incompetence," and the highest is a "6," which means almost native-like writing ability. Currently, the test is offered in September, October, March, and May. If you take the TOEFL during these months, you must take the TWE; it is not optional.

Exercise 15: Short Presentation

Study the following information. Put together a short, one-minute talk about the different kinds of doctors. You can refer to your notes but don't read them when you speak. Your teacher will choose one aspect (part) of pronunciation for you to focus on.

Physicians

There are many kinds of doctors who specialize in different areas. It is important to know the names of the different specialties when trying to find a doctor. Here are some of the more common ones:

Area

Dermatology	Dermatologists take care of the skin.
General Practice	G.P.'s* treat the whole family.
Gynecology	Gynecologists are for women.
Internal Medicine	Internists treat diseases in adults.
Neurology	Neurologists specialize in the brain.
Obstetrics	Obstetricians see pregnant women.
Ophthalmology	Ophthalmologists take care of the eye.
Orthopedics	Orthopedists specialize in bones.
Pediatrics	Pediatricians see children.
Psychiatry	Psychiatrists treat emotional illnesses.

Exercise 16: Picture Description

Say as much as you can about the picture in one minute.

*General Practitioner

12

Contractions

Part I: Contractions with "will"

(a) I'll see you. (b) She'll understand.	In spoken English, it is more common for "will" to be contracted than not. Note the pronunciation for contracted "will" with personal pronouns: I'll /al/ *ahl* you'll /yəl/ *yul* he'll /hɪl/ *hil* she'll /shɪl/ *shil* we'll /wəl/ *wul* they'll /ðəl/ *thul*
(c) What'll it be? (d) One'll do. (e) That'll be all.	Other contractions with "will" are as follows. what'll* when'll who'll how'll which'll where'll there'll it'll* one'll that'll*
(f) John'll go. (g) Nancy'll know.	It is very common in spoken English to contract "will" with names, as in (g) and (h). Note: these contractions are good practice for /l/.

*The /t/ is a flap sound.

Exercise 1: Listening

Circle "yes" if you hear a contraction with "will" and "no" if there is no contraction.

1. yes   no   4. yes   no

2. yes   no   5. yes   no

3. yes   no   6. yes   no

Exercise 2: Listening

Fill in the blanks with the words you hear.

1. _____ happen next?

2. _____ take time.

3. _____ be a few minutes late.

4. _____ check and see.

Check your answers.

5. _____ you be?

6. _____ never believe it.

7. If _____ do it, that's fine.

8. _____ never work.

Exercise 3: Listening and Production

Part A: Listen to the following sentences.

1. What'll I do?
   they say?
   we order?
   you get?
2. It'll work out.
   be O.K.
   never happen.
   be a surprise.
3. How'll you do it?
   we get there?
   you know?
   he find out?

4. That'll help.
        work.
        be all.
        be a miracle.

5. Who'll know?
        find out?
        go first?
        drive?

6. Where'll we meet?
            I buy it?
            they be?

7. We'll need more.
        see.
        be there.
        try.

Part B: With a partner, choose some of these sentences to practice.

Exercise 4: Listening and Production

Listen to the following sentences and practice pronouncing them.

1. We'll see about it later.
2. What'll you have?
3. That'll come later.
4. There'll be more to do.
5. I'll let you know.
6. It'll be a surprise.

It'll be a surprise.

Exercise 5: Production

With a partner, complete the sentences with words of your choice (keep them short), and practice pronouncing them.

1. We'll . . .
2. When'll . . .
3. There'll . . .
4. They'll . . .
5. Where'll . . .
6. I'll . . .
7. It'll . . .
8. You'll . . .

Part II: Contractions with the Verb "be"

(a) I'm leaving now. (b) You're right.	In relaxed speech, the contracted forms for "I" and "you" can change as follows: I'm /am/ *ahm* you're /yər/ *yer*
(c) We're ready.	"We're" can have the same pronunciation as the past tense verb "were" in relaxed speech.
(d) They're over there in their car.	"They're" is pronounced the same as "their" or "there."
(e) My cold's getting worse. (f) This one's ready. (g) Sam's here. (h) What's the next step?	Contractions with "is" are extremely common in spoken English.

Exercise 6: Listening

Circle "yes" if there is a contraction with the verb "be" and "no" if not.

1. yes   no

2. yes   no

3. yes   no

    4. yes   no

    5. yes   no

Check your answers.

    6. yes   no

    7. yes   no

    8. yes   no

    9. yes   no

   10. yes   no

Exercise 7: Listening

Fill in the blanks with the words you hear.

    1. That _____ not ready yet.

    2. _____ over

       _____.

    3. _____ planning to go.

    4. _____ looking a little nervous.

Check your answers.

    5. Your _____ certainly clean.

    6. _____ stuck in traffic.

    7. _____ already running late.

    8. I hear _____ getting divorced.

Exercise 8: Production

Practice pronouncing the following phrases.

    1. this one's O.K.   5. my cold's not
    2. I'm trying   6. John's never
    3. Kathy's sick   7. Pat's got
    4. we're looking   8. your friend's name

Exercise 9: Listening and Production

Listen to the following sentences and practice pronouncing them.

1. I'm trying to understand.
2. My cold's not getting better.
3. John's never late.
4. We're looking for a bigger apartment.
5. This one's not O.K.
6. Kathy's sick again today.

Exercise 10: Production

With a partner, complete the sentences with words of your choice (keep them short) and practice pronouncing them.

1. The test's . . .
2. They're . . .
3. You're . . .
4. Our teacher's . . .
5. (Partner's name) . . .
6. Your answer's . . .

Part III: Contractions with "have," "has," "does," "did"

(a) How've you been? (b) Who've we got? (c) What've we done?	In spoken English, contractions with wh-words + "have" are as follows: how've why've who've when've /əv/ where've what've /əv/
(d) I should have known. should/ə/ (e) He must have gone. must/ə/ (f) You could have asked. could/əv/ (g) They might have arrived. might/əv/	Modals are also commonly used with the contracted "have" in spoken English. If a consonant sound follows "have," "have" usually sounds like /ə/, as in (d) and (e). If a vowel follows "have," the reduction is usually /əv/, as in (f) and (g). If you make the /əv/ contraction, it is very important for /v/ to be heard, and correctly voiced.

(h) When's it arriving? (i) When's it arrive? (j) He's never been before. (k) Karen's got time.	"Is," "does" and "has" are frequently contracted in spoken English, as in (h)–(k). The main verb in the sentence will be the clue to the correct auxiliary verb.
(l) Where'd that happen? (m) Who'd do that?	"Did" is frequently contracted with wh-words in native speech, as in (l) and (m). Other contractions are as follows: how'd what'd /əd/ why'd when'd

Exercise 11: Listening

Circle "yes" if there is a contraction with "have," "has," "does," or "did," or a reduction with "have," and circle "no" if not.

1. yes   no

2. yes   no

3. yes   no

4. yes   no

Check your answers.

5. yes   no

6. yes   no

7. yes   no

8. yes   no

Exercise 12: Listening

Fill in the blanks with the missing words. (Write the long form.)

1. _____ done?

2. _____ found?

3. _____ ever said that?

4. _____ do that?

Check your answers.

5. _____ come.

6. _____ heard that before?

7. _____ look bad?

8. _____ figured that?

Exercise 13: Listening (Optional)

Circle the correct verb. (The verbs will be spoken in contracted form.)

1.	does	did	4.	does	did
2.	does	did	5.	does	did
3.	does	did	6.	does	did

Exercise 14: Production

Practice pronouncing the following phrases.

1. what've you
2. who've they
3. when've I
4. how'd you

5. why've we
6. where've we
7. I should've
8. how've you

Exercise 15: Listening and Production

Listen to the following sentences and practice pronouncing them.

1. What've you been up to?
2. I must've lost it.
3. When've I ever said that?
4. How'd they look?
5. Why've we come here?
6. Where've I heard that before?
7. Where's it say that?
8. How've they taken the news?

Exercise 16: Production

With a partner, complete the sentences with words of your choice (keep them short) and practice pronouncing them. Have your teacher check them first.

1. Why've . . .
2. Where've . . .
3. What've . . .
4. When's . . .
5. How've . . .
6. I _____ . . .
   (any past tense modal)
7. When've . . .
8. What'd . . .

Part IV: Contractions with "would" and "had"

(a) That'd be great.
        (would)
(b) It'd make sense.
        (would)
(c) That'd been done before.
        (had)
(d) It'd better be ready.
        (had)
	In spoken English, contractions with "would" and "had" are very common.
	
	The final **d** in these contractions actually has an additional syllable:
	
	    /əd/

(e) Jan'd go. (f) Bob'd know. (g) If Jack'd had time, he would have gone.	Note that names are also commonly contracted with "would" and "had" as in (e), (f), and (g).

Exercise 17: Listening

Circle "yes" if there is a contraction with "would" or "had" and "no" if not.

1. yes   no

2. yes   no

3. yes   no

4. yes   no

Check your answers.

5. yes   no

6. yes   no

7. yes   no

8. yes   no

Exercise 18: Listening

Circle the correct verb for the contracted form.

1. would   had

2. would   had

3. would   had

4. would   had

5. would   had

6. would   had

Exercise 19: Listening

Fill in the blanks with the words you hear. (Write the long forms.)

1. _____ be a step in the right direction.

2. _____ happen if I didn't go?

3. _____ happened was a mistake.

4. _____ tried to call.

5. _____ never occurred to me to ask.

6. If _____ seen what

_____ seen.

Exercise 20: Production

Practice pronouncing the following phrases.

1. that'd be
2. what'd happen
3. what'd happened
4. Dave'd try
5. it'd never occurred
6. if you'd seen

Exercise 21: Listening and Production

Listen to the following sentences and practice pronouncing them.

1. That'd be the best yet!
2. What'd happen if I didn't go?
3. What'd happened was that he got a flat tire.
4. Dave'd try to help out if he could.
5. It'd gone by so quickly that we didn't see it.
6. If you'd seen the look on her face.

Exercise 22: Sentence Completion

With a partner, complete the sentences with words of your choice (keep them short) and practice pronouncing them. Have your teacher check them first.

1. It'd . . .
2. The weather'd better . . .
3. How much'd . . .
4. (Partner's name) 'd . . .
5. If I'd known, . . .
6. This'd . . .

CHAPTER REVIEW

Exercise 23: Dialogue Practice

Practice the following dialogues with a partner. First, mark the linking and where you think sounds might change. Before you say your sentence, study it for a moment so that when you speak, you can look at your partner without reading. Remember to focus on the pronunciation of the contractions.

1. *A:* How's your paper coming?

   B: It's almost finished.

2. *A:* If I'd have had time, I would've helped.

   B: It'll all work out.

3. *A:* You must've known sooner.

   B: If I'd have known, you'd have known.

4. *A:* What'll it be?

   B: I think we'll split an order, but we're not quite ready.

5. *A:* What've you heard about her?

   B: That she'd be very organized.

6. *A:* Where'd you ever get that idea?

   B: What's wrong with it?

Exercise 24: Paragraph Reading

Read the following paragraph aloud. Before you begin, make sure you understand all the vocabulary. Ask your teacher or check your dictionary.

Doggie Bags

In the U.S. and Canada, if you eat out in restaurants frequently, you will sooner or later come across the idea of a "doggie bag." This refers to the custom which allows you to take home the food you ordered but cannot finish. Originally, restaurants had bags with the words "doggie bags" printed on them. The suggestion was that the food was to be given to the pet dog at home. (Of course, this was usually not the case.) Some people feel childish using this phrase and instead say to the waiter, "I'd like to take this home" or "I'd like to have this wrapped up." Your remaining food will be brought back in a container, for you to enjoy later. If you haven't tried this, don't be embarrassed. It's a common custom.

Exercise 25: Short Presentation

Study the following information. Using your own words, put together a short, one-minute talk about buying a used car. You can refer to your notes but don't read them when you speak. Your teacher will choose one aspect of pronunciation for you to focus on.

Buying a Used Car

1. Never buy a car the first time you go to the dealer. Sleep on your decision! If you don't trust yourself to take your time deciding, then leave your money at home. If the dealer tells you that you need to decide quickly or the car will be gone, just tell him/her, "That's O.K." This is a common sales argument that dealers use.

2. Check the *Blue Book* if available. This lists current car prices.

3. Ask the dealer to see the invoice (this shows the price that the *dealer* paid for the car). From this information you can decide if the selling price is fair. If the dealer won't show you the invoice, then go to another dealer.

4. Test drive the car. (Expect the dealer to tell you that it is wonderful.) Take it to a mechanic to have the engine checked, even if the outside of the car looks great! This might cost some money, but it will save you a lot of money if the engine has problems.

5. Remember that the price does not include tax and license, which can significantly increase the price of the car. It is also a good idea to call an insurance agent to find out what the cost of insurance will be. Newer sports cars, for example, might cost at least $1,000 per year to insure.

6. If the dealer promises you anything, make sure he or she writes it down on paper.

Exercise 26: Interview

Part A: Interview two native speakers of English. Write their answers in the blanks, and remember to have them sign their names. When asking your questions, focus especially on the contractions studied in this chapter. Study each question before you speak so that you do not have to read it. You may want to practice with a partner first.

1. What'll you do tonight?
2. What've you got planned for tomorrow?
3. Where've you never been?
4. What'd happen if you moved away from here?
5. How'll you feel in 20 years?
6. How'd you act if you were elected president or prime minister?
7. Where'll you be next year?
8. What would you do if you'd suddenly won a lot of money?
9. Who's been the most important person in your life?
10. Why've you decided to answer these questions?

Answers:

1.	1.
2.	2.
3.	3.
4.	4.
5.	5.
6.	6.
7.	7.
8.	8.
9.	9.
10.	10.

_____   _____
      (signature)   (signature)

Part B: Report your answers to the class or small group your teacher assigns.

Exercise 27: Picture Description

Say as much as you can about the picture in one minute.

APPENDIX A

Consonant Practice

/b/ and /p/

Articulation: −lips together
                    −voiced for /b/
                    −voiceless for /p/

Sound focus: Press your lips lightly together. Let the air build up behind them and then release it.

/b/

bad	lab	business
obey	busy	taxicab
able	between	about
bathtub	because	behavior
club	subway	rib

1. Bob's unable to obey.
2. Are you going by cab or subway?
3. Both businesses are broke.
4. Buy between December and February.

/p/

Pat	lap	stop
perform	trip	develop
punish	step	paper
picture	opinion	operate
pan	open	pepper

1. Open the package please.
2. Don't step on the picture.
3. Which parking place?
4. I'll get the pictures developed.

Tip: To test whether air is coming out when you pronounce /p/, place a piece of paper in front of your lips. When you say /p/, the paper should move from the puff of air. When you say /b/, there should be no movement. This works for /p/ at the beginning of a word, or for /p/ that begins a syllable (e.g. opinion).

/v/ and /f/

Articulation: −upper teeth lightly placed on lower lip
    −lower lip **does not** move when you force out the air
    −/v/ is voiced
    −/f/ is voiceless

Sound focus: (Close your eyes.) Place your upper teeth gently on your lower lip. Let them lightly rest there. Force out some air. The teeth should still be touching the lips to create friction. Make sure the lower lip stays still.

Feel your throat for the /v/. There should be vibration. Move between /v/ and /f/ and feel the vibration stop and start as you do this. Both these sounds can continue for a long time.

/v/

very	of	behavior
alive	oven	receive
invite	video	television
five	average	TV
seven	VCR	expensive

1. I have five invitations.
2. The average age is seven.
3. This TV is very expensive.
4. The vegetables are in the oven.

/f/

unfair	laugh	favorite
perfect	if	difference
family	cough	traffic
perfume	off	physician
effect	often	fix

1. Fix the furnace.
2. I'm off for the first week.
3. What effect on the future will more traffic have?
4. I couldn't tell if that was a laugh or a cough.

/d/ and /t/

Articulation: —tip of tongue briefly touches bump behind
            upper teeth
        —voiced for /d/
        —voiceless for /t/

Sound focus: (Close your eyes). Feel the area behind your upper front teeth with your tongue. Pull your tongue slightly back. You will feel a bump behind your teeth. Move your tongue around this area. Let it rest. Let some air build up behind your tongue. Release it. Just let your tongue drop a little rather than pushing it forward or pulling it down.

/d/

mad	body	added
made	dial	sad
confused	wonderful	mud
day	disk	deep
dumb	add	Don

1. Dan did it already.
2. He acted sad, not mad.

3. Did Dad's doctor sound confused?
4. Don't drive in the mud.

/t/

tape	time	pet
Tom	might	tax
bought	suntan	attack
tell	got	meat
wet	stopped	terrible

1. He paid the extra tax.
2. I added two to the list.
3. Did Tom tell you to do that?
4. Take the video cassette.

/g/ and /k/

Articulation: —back of tongue stops air against back of throat
                —voiced for /g/
                —voiceless for /k/

Sound focus: (Close your eyes.) Press the back part of your tongue firmly against the back part of your throat. Let the air build up behind this block. (It will feel a little like you are choking!) Drop your tongue (and jaw) slightly and let the air push through. This will make a /g/ or /k/.

/k/

cash	luck	occasion
can	drink	backache
cure	occur	doctor
action	awkward	acquire
unique	catalog	joke

1. It was an awkward joke.
2. How about seeing the doctor for your backache?
3. Will it be cash or check?
4. Everyone in the back of the car must buckle up.

/g/

good	green	leg
guest	agree	plug
gun	burger	ugly
great	drug	got
ago	big	Greg

1. He gave up cigarettes and cigars.
2. I forgot how great a burger can taste.
3. Good grief! Eggs again?
4. The girls have got guests coming in August.

sh /ʃ/ and zh /ʒ/

Articulation: —the sides of the tongue against the sides of the upper teeth
—tongue curled up
—lips rounded
—*sh* is voiceless
—*zh* is voiced

Sound focus: (Close your eyes.) Place the sides of your tongue against the sides of your upper back teeth. But leave a space between the front of your tongue and the ridge (bumpy part) behind your front teeth for the air to pass through. Round your lips. Let the air pass over the groove in the middle of the tongue. Make sure your lips stay rounded. Both *sh* and *zh* can continue for a long time.

sh /ʃ/

she	attention	wish
share	lecture	permission
action	wash	patient
fish	ashes	national
crash	sugar	Chicago

1. She wishes her patience weren't so short.
2. The crash in Chicago made national news.
3. The social issues lecture didn't catch my attention.
4. She should see his facial expressions.

zh /ʃ/

occasionally	confusion	leisure
garage	massage	pleasure
measure	television	invasion
decision	usually	beige
casual	corsage	revision

1. The television is usually off before midnight.
2. Occasionally I get a massage to relax.
3. Measure the beige carpet.
4. That garage doesn't do any collision work.

ch /tʃ/ and j /dz/

Articulation: —tip of tongue touches upper tooth ridge
—sides of tongue against sides of upper teeth
—lips rounded
—ch is voiceless
—j is voiced

Sound focus: (Close your eyes.) Put the front of your tongue firmly along the ridge (bumpy part) behind your upper front teeth. Round your lips. Let the air build up behind this block. Then release the tip of the tongue, but keep the sides of the tongue touching against the tooth ridge as the air goes out. Be careful not to slide your tongue forward on the tooth ridge; rather, let it drop.

Tip: For *ch*, think of making a *sh* with a *t* to stop the air.

For *j*, think of making a *zh* with a *d* to stop the air.

ch /tʃ/

choose	ketchup	furniture
check	children	situation
chicken	kitchen	fortunately
H	watch	Chinese
match	temperature	pinch

1. There's some Chinese fortune cookies in the kitchen.
2. Why didn't you check the child's temperature?
3. Is there ketchup on my chin?
4. Which furniture did they choose, the cheap stuff?

j /dʒ/

just	jungle	page
jacket	schedule	gradually
message	individually	luggage
judge	language	college
June	gym	injure

1. He got the injury in college.
2. I'll leave a message at the gym.
3. He majored in languages.
4. Schedule it for June or July.

/w/

Articulation: −rounded lips

Sound focus: (Close your eyes.) Round your lips into a tight, small circle. They should almost be closed. Feel your tongue pull back and high so that it is almost ready to touch the back of the throat to make a /g/. This is the position for /w/.

Tip: The vowel sounds that follow /w/ all make the lips open widely. Say "we," "when," "walk," and "would."

/w/

want	wipe	one
woman	worry	would
women	sweep	wood
away	sweater	language
unwed	between	were

1. Wipe away your tears and wave good-bye.
2. We weren't aware that we were being watched.
3. Would you like this sweater or that one?
4. Do women in your country worry about being unwed?

/y/

Articulation: —middle of tongue close to the hard palate (the middle of the roof of your mouth)
—sides of tongue touching back teeth

Sound focus: (Close your eyes.) Put the tip of your tongue against the inside of your bottom teeth. Raise the middle of your tongue near (but not touching) your hard palate.

Make sure that the sides of your tongue are touching the sides of your upper back teeth. Move them around a little to get the feeling. When you are ready to make a /y/, these sides will move forward a little. Your lips will be relaxed and a little open. This is the position for /y/.

Tip: The tongue tip never touches the top of the mouth, or else you will get a /j/-like sound. As you move from the /y/ into a following vowel, the tongue glides smoothly forward and down into the vowel, as in "year," "yes," and "yeah."

/y/

yes	university	cure
yesterday	U.S.	cucumber
yeah	use	few
union	usual	billion
yellow	cute	onion

1. Have you joined the union yet?
2. There's cucumber and yellow onion in the salad.
3. You used that excuse yesterday.
4. In the U.S., unlike Europe, a billion is a thousand millions.

/h/

Articulation: The exact position of the lips and tongue as the air blows out changes according to the sound that follows the /h/.

Sound focus: (Close your eyes.) Relax your lips and open them a little. Blow air from your lungs out through your mouth. The /h/ sound is this blowing air.

/h/

heavy	help	hair
human	unhappy	here
humor	perhaps	unhelpful
house	childhood	horrible
hold	uh-huh	hundred

1. Hello, can you hear me?
2. He had an unhappy childhood.
3. Who is responsible for her horrible haircut?
4. I hope they have hamburgers and hotdogs.

/m/

Articulation: —lips placed together

Sound focus: (Close your eyes.) The /m/ sound comes out your nose when your lips are closed together. Your mouth will open for the following vowel sound. The /m/ is a voiced sound. Put your hand on your throat to feel it vibrate.

/m/

make	game	empty
maybe	time	summer
male	admire	employee
female	imagine	grammar
aim	item	somebody

1. My employees don't make much money.
2. Is the animal male or female?
3. Maybe we can make time this morning to meet.
4. Wait a minute, I'm coming.

/n/

Articulation: —front of your tongue against upper tooth ridge

Sound focus: (Close your eyes.) Touch the front of your tongue firmly along the ridge behind your upper front teeth. Rest it on the bump. Make the /n/ sound come out your nose.

Tip: Compared with other languages, English /n/ uses a longer area of contact between the front of the tongue and the tooth ridge. Don't just use the tip of your tongue. Your tongue should be touching firmly along the whole ridge, behind all your front teeth.

/n/

nail	announce	burn
on	in	candy
not	near	man
under	interest	negative
enjoy	neck	naked

1. We're not at all interested in canoeing.
2. There's a burn ban on.
3. Our nearest neighbor is nine miles away.
4. The movie's not on 'till noon.

/ŋ/

Sound focus: (Close your eyes.) Open your lips a little. Touch the back of your tongue to the back of the top of your mouth (the soft palate), as if you were going to say a /g/, but make the sound come out your nose. There will be voicing.

Note: This sound does not occur in English at the beginnings of words. Also, the letters *ng* do not always represent the sound /ŋ/. For example, *ng* is pronounced as /nj/ in "stranger," "ginger," and "engine." In "longer," "stronger," "hunger," and "younger," the sound is /ŋg/.

/ŋ/

bank	thinking
going	thank
coming	rank
thing	blank
think	drank

1. Are you coming or going?
2. What do you think about that bank?
3. My mind is blank.
4. I'm thinking about how to thank her.

APPENDIX B

Minimal Pair Practice with Consonants

b/p

1. bad/pad
2. lab/lap
3. rib/rip
4. bees/peas
5. cab/cap
6. cub/cup
7. ban/pan
8. lib/lip

b/v

1. ban/van
2. b/v
3. lib/live
4. berry/very
5. bow/vow
6. bowel/vowel
7. back/vac
8. curb/curve

f/p

1. fit/pit
2. fat/pat
3. fad/pad
4. laugh/lap
5. cuff/cup
6. suffer/supper
7. coffee/copy
8. cough/cop

f/v

1. life/live
2. fan/van
3. fairy/very
4. feign/vein
5. folly/volley
6. belief/believe
7. infest/invest
8. thief/thieve

f/h

1. food/who'd
2. fizz/his
3. fail/hail
4. fool/who'll
5. fell/hell
6. fee/he
7. fate/hate
8. fall/hall

f/θ

1. fink/think
2. fret/threat
3. Fred/thread
4. laugh/lath
5. deaf/death
6. miff/myth
7. frill/thrill
8. first/thirst

s/sh

1. see/she
2. Sue/shoe
3. seed/she'd
4. sip/ship
5. plus/plush
6. Paris/parish
7. gas/gash
8. crass/crash

sh/ch

1. wish/which
2. wash/watch
3. ship/chip
4. share/chair
5. mush/much
6. hush/hutch
7. washed/watched
8. washing/watching

sh/j

1. marsh/Marge
2. martian/margin
3. slush/sludge
4. bash/badge
5. sheep/jeep
6. shade/jade
7. Shelly/jelly
8. sham/jam

t/d

1. two/do
2. tale/Dale
3. tall/doll
4. ought/odd
5. cart/card
6. let/led
7. hat/had
8. tie/die

t/p

1. top/pop
2. type/pipe
3. test/pest
4. cat/cap
5. cot/cop
6. write/ripe
7. flat/flap
8. mat/map

d/z

1. do/zoo
2. doom/zoom
3. doomed/zoomed
4. dooms/zooms
5. dip/zip
6. dipper/zipper
7. made/maze
8. had/has

d/j

1. dale/jail
2. dig/jig
3. dim/Jim
4. deep/jeep
5. deli/jelly
6. lard/large
7. wade/wage
8. dunk/junk

d/r

1. damp/ramp
2. diet/riot
3. dock/rock
4. road/roar
5. bed/bear
6. head/hair
7. hid/hear
8. code/core

θ/t

1. thin/tin
2. thinker/tinker
3. thorn/torn
4. thought/taught
5. bath/bat
6. math/mat
7. thank/tank
8. with/wit

θ/sh

1. thin/shin
2. thank/shank
3. through/shrew
4. with/wish
5. lath/lash
6. math/mash
7. thrill/shrill
8. throw/show

θ/s

1. thick/sick
2. thud/sud
3. thin/sin
4. bath/bass
5. math/mass
6. thank/sank
7. mouth/mouse
8. path/pass

θ/ð

1. mouth/mouthe
2. thigh/thy
3. teeth/teethe
4. ether/either

ð/d

1. they/day
2. father/fodder
3. then/den
4. those/doze
5. than/Dan
6. there/dare
7. though/doe
8. bathe/bade

ð/z

1. then/Zen
2. breathe/breeze
3. clothe/close
4. clothing/closing
5. thee/Z
6. seething/seizing
7. soothe/Sue's
8. clothed/closed

g/k

1. dog/dock
2. frog/frock
3. log/lock
4. mug/muck
5. pig/pick
6. gap/cap
7. grate/crate
8. bag/back

v/w

1. very/wary
2. grove/grow
3. viper/wiper
4. verse/worse
5. stove/stow
6. move/moo
7. vine/wine
8. vile/while

v/ð

1. veil/they'll
2. vat/that
3. van/than
4. clove/clothe
5. live/lithe
6. sliver/slither
7. V/thee
8. loaves/loathes

v/z

1. vest/zest
2. I've/eyes
3. carve/cars
4. dove/does
5. shelve/shells
6. novel/nozzle
7. drive/dries
8. arrive/arise

ch/j

1. chalk/jock
2. cheap/jeep
3. match/Madge
4. rich/ridge
5. batch/badge
6. choke/joke
7. chunk/junk
8. etching/edging

y/j

1. yell/jail
2. yet/jet
3. yak/Jack
4. yacht/jot
5. yolk/joke
6. year/jeer
7. yard/jarred
8. yellow/Jello

w/r

1. wait/rate
2. tow/tore
3. wipe/ripe
4. wide/ride
5. mow/more
6. stow/store
7. away/array
8. west/rest

n/ŋ

1. gone/gong
2. lawn/long
3. pin/ping
4. wins/wings
5. runs/rungs
6. stun/stung
7. fan/fang
8. sinner/singer

n/l

1. not/lot
2. Ned/led
3. nab/lab
4. nick/lick
5. need/lead
6. Nate/late
7. know/low
8. knob/lob

APPENDIX C

Minimal Pair Practice with Vowels

I/iy

1. fill/feel
2. pit/Pete
3. been/bean
4. hid/heed
5. biz/bees
6. Liz/Lee's
7. sin/scene
8. pill/peel
9. pip/peep
10. his/he's

ε/æ

1. set/sat
2. bread/Brad
3. fret/frat
4. blend/bland
5. den/Dan
6. mess/mass
7. met/mat
8. pest/passed
9. said/sad
10. lend/land

ε/ey

1. met/mate
2. red/raid
3. sell/sail
4. wetter/waiter
5. yell/Yale
6. wet/wait
7. red/raid
8. sent/saint
9. men/main
10. pepper/paper

ε/a

1. bet/bought
2. less/loss
3. red/rod
4. deck/dock
5. bend/bond
6. neck/knock
7. set/sought
8. sex/socks
9. Ned/nod
10. get/got

I/ɛ

1. did/dead
2. bin/Ben
3. knit/net
4. Rick/wreck
5. hill/hell
6. pit/pet
7. fill/fell
8. disk/desk
9. rid/red
10. wind/wend

æ/a

1. Dan/Don
2. fat/fought
3. ran/Ron
4. cat/caught
5. sad/sod
6. band/bond
7. Jan/John
8. gnat/not
9. Al/all
10. last/lost

ey/æ

1. mate/mat
2. fate/fat
3. plane/plan
4. rain/ran
5. pale/pal
6. main/man
7. hate/hat
8. Dale/Dan
9. sail/Sal
10. made/mad

ə/a

1. pup/pop
2. sub/sob
3. muss/moss
4. cut/caught
5. rut/rot
6. gun/gone
7. lust/lost
8. but/bought
9. cup/cop
10. color/collar

ɛ/ə

1. met/mutt
2. get/gut
3. den/done
4. lest/lust
5. pen/pun
6. rent/runt
7. fend/fund
8. beg/bug
9. meg/mug
10. when/won

I/ey

1. mit/mate
2. mid/made
3. itch/H
4. will/wale
5. his/haze
6. mill/male
7. pill/pale
8. gin/Jane
9. pin/pain
10. hill/hale

I/ə

1. pin/pun
2. bid/bud
3. mist/must
4. fin/fun
5. win/won
6. list/lust
7. big/bug
8. kiss/cuss
9. din/done
10. miss/muss

a/ow

1. not/note
2. on/own
3. cost/coast
4. want/won't
5. fawn/phone
6. mall/mole
7. cod/code
8. tot/tote
9. doll/dole
10. dot/dote

æ/ə

1. cap/cup
2. fan/fun
3. bad/bud
4. dad/dud
5. cat/cut
6. dance/dunce
7. lamp/lump
8. Sam/some
9. mat/mutt
10. clamp/clump

ə/ʊ

1. buck/book
2. luck/look
3. tuck/took
4. shuck/shook
5. putt/put

ə/ow

1. must/most
2. dove/dove
3. suck/soak
4. rut/wrote
5. but/boat
6. cup/cope
7. flood/flowed
8. dumb/dome
9. bust/boast
10. cussed/coast

ey/a

1. late/lot
2. tape/top
3. fate/fought
4. tail/tall
5. lane/lawn
6. gain/gone
7. mail/mall
8. cane/con
9. Dane/Don
10. rake/rock

a/aw

1. shot/shout
2. loss/louse
3. bond/bound
4. clot/clout
5. fond/found
6. gone/gown
7. got/gout
8. pot/pout
9. bought/bout
10. clod/cloud

APPENDIX D

General Rules for Predicting Stress (with Supplemental Practice)

Unfortunately, rules for English stress are very complex. When you learn a new word, you will generally have to learn its stress by listening carefully to a native speaker or by looking it up in a dictionary.

However, there are a few rules that can usually be followed for stress placement. (But don't be disappointed if later you find a few exceptions to these rules.)

1. Most two-syllable words are stressed on the first syllable:

   ́awful   ́never

2. With words that can be both nouns and verbs, or verbs and adjectives, stress will usually fall on the SECOND syllable if the word is a VERB:

   rec ́ord   perf ́ect

   If the word is a noun or adjective, stress falls on the FIRST syllable:

   r ́ecord   p ́erfect

205

3. Compound nouns (two nouns put together to make one word) are usually stressed on the first syllable:

   ´airport   ´freeway

4. Two-word verbs are stressed on the second word:

   go a´way   get ´up

5. In three-syllable words, stress usually falls on the first or second syllable:

   be´autiful   um´brella

Note: As you have learned, unstressed syllables can be reduced to /ə/. Sometimes, however, when the stress falls on the first syllable, the vowel in the last syllable is not reduced. This pattern of two full syllables is common:

   ´hurri\cane   ´demon\strate

6. When a suffix (ending) is added to a word, the stress usually doesn't change:

   ´open   → ´openness
   ´hospital → ´hospitalize

   Exceptions to this include the following endings:

   -ic, -ical, -tion, -ity
   ´drama   → dra´matic

Supplementary Practice

A. Listen to the different stress in the following verb and not-verb pairs.

Verb	Not Verb
1. pre´sent	´present
2. permit	permit
3. conflict	conflict
4. perfect	perfect

5. conduct   conduct
6. increase   increase
7. protest   protest
8. insult   insult

Practice pronouncing these pairs. Remember to reduce the unstressed syllables to /ə/ where needed.

B. Mark the stressed syllable in each underlined word in the sentences below. Refer to the list in A if you need to.

1. The students set a new record for perfect attendance, for which they were presented good conduct medals.

2. Sorry, you need a parking permit for this lot.

3. Does water contract when it freezes, or does its volume increase?

4. A: I know he insulted you, but don't start a conflict with him or throw any insults back at him, because he's your boss.

   B: But I want to protest his conduct. He shouldn't be permitted to act that way. Besides, I have a contract so he can't fire me.

Listen to these sentences. Then, practice reading them with a partner.

C. Listen to the following three-syllable words. Decide if the stress is on the first or second syllable. Mark the stressed syllable.

1. government   5. expensive

2. curious   6. document

3. vanilla   7. commercial

4. delicate   8. popular

Listen again to the pronunciation of these words. Notice that the unstressed syllables are all reduced. Practice pronouncing them.

D. Listen to the following three-syllable words. Notice that the stress is on the first syllable, the middle syllable is reduced, but the last syllable is NOT reduced to /ə/.

1. crocodile   5. envelope
2. hurricane   6. telegram
3. decorate   7. photograph
4. advertise   8. organize

Practice pronouncing these words with a partner. Then, take turns asking your partner a question using a word from the list. Your partner will answer your question.

E. Listen to the pronunciation of the following compound nouns.

1. notebook   6. haircut
2. newspaper   7. traffic light
3. backache   8. bus stop
4. classroom   9. vacuum cleaner
5. water softener   10. x-ray machine

Now practice pronouncing them with stress on the first part.

F. Listen to the following conversations. Mark the stress in the underlined compound nouns and two-word verbs.

1. *A:* Does this bus go to the <u>airport</u>?

    B: Yes, but you have to <u>get off</u> at the <u>bus stop</u> downtown on Pike Street. Then, <u>get on</u> the Number 27 there. Or you can catch a <u>taxicab</u> on any <u>street corner</u>, but it's much more expensive.

2. *A:* If you get to the <u>classroom</u> late, please <u>come in</u> and <u>sit down</u> quietly. You don't need to knock on the door or apologize.

    B: O.K. Thanks for <u>pointing</u> that <u>out</u>. In my country, customs are very different. For example, students always have to <u>stand up</u> when the teacher <u>comes in</u>. It's much more formal.

3. *A:* I'm going shopping. What else do we need? I'm also <u>going</u>
to the <u>drugstore</u>.

    B: <u>Dish soap</u>, <u>toothpaste</u>, <u>hairspray</u>, <u>cough syrup</u>, <u>dog food</u>, <u>ice
cream</u>; . . . and would you get me a <u>flashlight</u>, some cheap
<u>sunglasses</u>, and a <u>can opener</u>? Oh, and a <u>newspaper</u>, too.

    A: You bet. That should keep me busy!

4. *A:* I have too much <u>homework</u> tonight, so I can't <u>come over</u>.
And could I borrow your <u>notebook</u>? I'll <u>give</u> it <u>back</u>
tomorrow.

    B: Sure. But if you finish and can <u>get away</u> for some fun later,
<u>drop by</u>, because I'll be <u>staying up</u> really late watching two
<u>videotapes</u>.

With a partner, practice reading the conversations. Then choose
one conversation to practice until it feels smooth and comfortable
to read.

G. Look at the sets of related words. Their roots are the same, but
they have different grammatical endings (suffixes). Think about
how to pronounce them and see if you can correctly mark the
stressed syllable in each word.

1. photograph	photography	photographer	photographic
2. electric	electrify	electricity	electrical
3. cooperate	cooperative	cooperation	
4. modern	modernize	modernity	
5. history	historian	historical	historically
6. science	scientist	scientific	

Listen again to these words and repeat them, paying special attention to making the stressed syllables longer and higher in pitch,
while using /ə/ in syllables that are reduced.

With a partner, take turns pronouncing these related sets of words.
Check each other's pronunciation of stressed and reduced syllables.

H. Sometimes, a suffix can cause the stress to change. These suffixes include *-ic, -ical, -tion,* and *-ity.*

Listen to the following sets of words. Notice that the stress in column A is different from column B. In column B, the syllable BEFORE the suffix is stressed.

A	B
1. drama	dramatic
2. psychology	psychological
3. active	activity
4. specialize	specialization
5. apologize	apologetic
6. mechanism	mechanic

I. Interview two native speakers of English. Ask them the following questions. Take notes on their answers and be ready to report on them in class. You may want to practice with a partner first. Be careful to stress the underlined words correctly.

1. What kind of <u>personality</u> did your favorite teacher during your elementary or <u>high school education</u> have? What do you think are important qualities for <u>a good educator</u> (teacher) to have?

2. Many people are worried that we are destroying our <u>environment</u>. In your opinion, what are two things that <u>humanity</u> (people in the world) should do to protect our world for future generations?

3. What do you think <u>represents</u> one of the most <u>dramatic</u> happenings in the world since you were born? How about the most <u>dramatic</u> happening within the last year or two? Why?

4. Many countries are <u>generating electrical energy</u> with nuclear power. Do you think that there are better sources of <u>electricity</u> than nuclear power? Do you think that we should <u>abolish</u> (get rid of) nuclear power? Why or why not?

5. If you didn't have enough money and had to <u>economize</u>, what would be the easiest way for you to live more <u>economically</u> and save money? What would be the most difficult thing for you to give up?

6. When a couple gets married or agrees to live together, what kinds of things do they often need to <u>negotiate</u> about their life together? What kinds of things most often cause <u>disagreements</u>?

Transcripts for Listening Exercises

CHAPTER 2

Exercise 1

1. Dan/Don
2. add/I'd
3. an/an
4. fan/fun
5. blank/blank
6. Joan/Jan
7. shatter/shatter
8. plaid/plaid
9. John/Jan
10. mutter/matter

Exercise 2

1. backs/backs/bucks
2. racket/racket/rocket
3. lope/lap/lap
4. drank/drank/drunk
5. snake/snack/snack
6. possible/passible/passible
7. than/then/than
8. add/add/odd
9. dead/dad/dad
10. bought/bat/bat

Exercise 7

1. feel/fill
2. bit/bit
3. this/this
4. live/love
5. cheap/chip
6. he's/his
7. win/won
8. fit/feet
9. well/will
10. dead/did

Exercise 8

1. knit/neat/knit
2. well/will/will
3. ring/rang/ring
4. fill/fill/feel
5. dead/did/did
6. sex/six/six
7. his/his/he's
8. each/itch/itch
9. live/leave/live
10. mull/mill/mill

Exercise 13

1. ten/ten
2. slept/slapped
3. mate/met
4. done/den
5. den/den
6. crept/creeped
7. debt/debt
8. money/many
9. left/left
10. deaf/deaf

Exercise 14

1. pen/pen/pan
2. won/when/when
3. late/let/let
4. bet/beat/bet
5. hail/hell/hell
6. shell/she'll/shell
7. met/met/meet
8. wail/well/well
9. bun/Ben/Ben
10. Sal/sell/sell

Exercise 19

1. Dan/Don
2. bomb/bomb
3. on/on
4. body/buddy
5. pot/pout
6. Joan/John
7. shot/shot
8. clod/cloud
9. slap/slop
10. got/goat

Exercise 20

1. box/box/bucks
2. rocket/racket/rocket
3. pup/pop/pop
4. calm/come/calm
5. shot/shot/shout
6. moss/moss/mouse
7. less/loss/loss
8. loss/louse/loss
9. shot/shot/shoot
10. note/not/not

Exercise 25

Part A

1. rock
2. pot
3. college
4. monster
5. lost
6. shock
7. doll
8. spot
9. hot dog
10. modern
11. hospital
12. sorry

Part B

1. father
2. bald
3. tall
4. far
5. water
6. hard
7. talk
8. large
9. law
10. awful

11. park
12. saw
13. barn
14. always
15. lawn

Part C

1. laundry
2. taught
3. daughter
4. fault
5. bought
6. fought
7. caught
8. automatic
9. cause
10. ought
11. cough
12. August

Exercise 27

1. off
2. call
3. taught
4. fond
5. lawn
6. common
7. bomb
8. popular
9. odd
10. blonde
11. Don
12. loss

Exercise 28

1. suit/soot
2. put/put
3. fool/full
4. would/wood
5. look/look
6. hood/who'd
7. bush/bush
8. could/cooed
9. stood/stood
10. shoed/should

Exercise 29

1. sought/soot/soot
2. could/could/cooed
3. put/putt/put
4. foot/foot/food
5. posh/push/push
6. buck/book/book
7. pull/pool/pull
8. shook/shook/shock
9. ball/bull/bull
10. nook/nuke/nook

CHAPTER 3
Exercise 1

1. my/pot/bright
2. geese/twice/guide
3. wipe/child/loyal
4. drive/heat/hide
5. strong/price/stripe
6. bound/bond/proud
7. dot/doubt/cloud
8. our/are/hour
9. drown/draw/vowel
10. pride/proud/shout
11. joint/noisy/north
12. boys/tease/toy
13. avoid/appoint/avow
14. coat/oil/coin
15. voted/poison/voyage

Exercise 6

1. leaving/leaving
2. sleep/slip
3. eat/eat
4. hit/heat
5. neat/nit
6. steal/steal
7. green/grin
8. itch/each
9. field/failed
10. leaking/leaking

Exercise 7

1. hate/heat/heat
2. tree/tree/tray
3. weed/wed/weed
4. well/wheel/wheel
5. easy/icy/easy
6. fees/fizz/fees
7. same/seem/seem
8. lip/leap/leap
9. eat/ate/eat
10. cheek/cheek/check

Exercise 12

1. beat/bait
2. late/late
3. tell/tale
4. greet/great
5. snake/snake
6. give/gave
7. taste/taste
8. run/rain
9. plane/plan
10. straight/straight

Exercise 13

1. may/me/may
2. steak/steak/stack
3. fell/fail/fail
4. laid/lid/laid
5. shape/shape/sheep
6. played/played/plead
7. bran/brain/brain
8. wet/wait/wait
9. age/age/edge
10. mail/meal/mail

Exercise 18

1. soup/soap
2. two/two
3. suit/soot
4. noon/noon
5. threw/through
6. towel/tool
7. fool/full
8. know/knew
9. smooth/smooth
10. spoon/spoon

Exercise 19

1. skull/school/school
2. fool/full/fool
3. stewed/stood/stewed
4. throw/threw/threw
5. bouts/boots/boots
6. cool/cool/coal
7. would/wooed/wooed
8. sued/sod/sued
9. root/wrote/root
10. puddle/poodle/poodle

Exercise 24

1. know/know
2. soak/sock
3. hop/hope
4. whole/whole
5. coast/coast
6. moaned/mound
7. both/both
8. tone/town
9. caught/coat
10. blown/blown

Exercise 25

1. note/note/nut
2. cop/cope/cope
3. bull/bowl/bowl
4. sewn/sewn/soon
5. toll/tall/toll
6. goat/got/goat
7. howl/hole/hole
8. both/both/booth
9. now/no/no
10. hop/hope/hope

CHAPTER 4

Exercise 1

1. fizz/fizz
2. Sue/zoo
3. days/days
4. face/face
5. muzzle/muscle
6. buss/buzz

Exercise 2

1. pays/pace/pace
2. Sue/Sue/zoo
3. ice/eyes/eyes
4. lacy/lazy/lacy
5. rise/rice/rise
6. zap/sap/sap
7. price/prize/price
8. plays/plays/place

Exercise 14

1. lake/rake
2. clown/crown
3. Neal/Neal
4. play/pray
5. raw/raw
6. right/right
7. bare/bale
8. stole/stole
9. mole/more
10. ray/lay

Exercise 15

1. lay/lay/ray
2. ball/bar/bar
3. lip/lip/rip
4. lent/rent/rent
5. mire/mile/mile
6. supplies/surprise/surprise
7. praise/praise/plays
8. loss/Ross/loss
9. race/race/lace
10. lap/wrap/lap

Exercise 31

1. play/plate
2. dad/dad
3. load/low
4. pawed/pot
5. mad/mad
6. pop/pop

Exercise 32

1. draw
2. stay
3. drop
4. wait
5. stayed
6. log

CHAPTER 5

Exercise 2

1. off and on
2. all over
3. in an hour
4. Am I
5. order coffee or
6. now or never
7. all
8. come again
9. for a
10. as if

CHAPTER 6

Exercise 6

1. cotton
2. eaten
3. sentence
4. fattening
5. getting
6. beaten
7. Something's
8. Certain
9. carton
10. mountain

Exercise 10

1. You can't be serious!
2. That can't work.
3. What can we do about it?
4. It can make a big difference.
5. Why can't she do it?
6. You can try harder.
7. That can't be right.
8. Things can change.
9. I can't argue with you.
10. I can't say enough about it.*

*Idiom = It's great, wonderful.

Exercise 11

1. can
2. Can't
3. can't
4. can
5. can
6. Can't
7. can
8. can't
9. can
10. Can

CHAPTER 7

Exercise 3

1. he
2. her
3. had
4. have
5. her
6. his
7. had
8. he

Exercise 4

1. he
2. her
3. his
4. had
5. have
6. has
7. have
8. his

Exercise 7

1. want to come
2. going to end
3. has to stay
4. have to find out
5. going to
6. have to have
7. has to be
8. going to want to know

Exercise 13

1. One of us
2. All of the
3. out-of-state
4. Some of that
5. waste of time
6. point of that
7. dollar's worth of
8. out of

Exercise 18

1. and
2. and
3. for/for
4. or
5. and

Exercise 19

1. or
2. and
3. or
4. and
5. and

CHAPTER 8
Exercise 7

1. child/head/table
2. When/flying/Mexico
3. class/20/students
4. sleep/bigger
5. this/mine
6. already done
7. Why/boss
8. promises/driving/fast

CHAPTER 9
Exercise 19

1. It's fun to see, Jack.
2. How much are you paying Jill?
3. How can you see Bill?
4. They are studying, Dr. Robb.
5. She bet Sue.
6. It's hard to judge Ms. Brown.
7. It's boring to watch, Gail.
8. How are you helping, Kelly?

CHAPTER 10
Exercise 1

1. What instrument do you play?
2. I never study.
3. It is filled with chocolate.
4. It was misplaced.

5. They added incorrectly.
6. I already asked.
7. He said they cried.
8. It started early.
9. What happened?
10. I really tried hard.

Exercise 9

1. waits
2. says
3. cars
4. makes
5. stories
6. causes
7. days
8. buses
9. sentences
10. drives

Exercise 18

1. 40 should be just right.
2. I need 15 more.
3. He's about 50 pounds overweight.
4. Did you say "16 miles"?
5. Eighteen-year-olds can't do that.
6. Thirty's a good age.

Exercise 19

1. 17 people were invited.
2. I think 80 will do.
3. Did you say 14 dollars?
4. Is 15 too many?
5. I guess 90 sounds about right.

CHAPTER 11
Exercise 1

1. risks
2. weakest subject
3. tasks
4. artists
5. tenths
6. rests
7. Is that
8. strengths
9. wrist's
10. Is there

Exercise 5

1. intermission
2. dental
3. quantity
4. winter
5. plenty
6. count on

CHAPTER 12
Exercise 1

1. Where will you be?
2. When'll she come?
3. Tom'll do it.
4. That'll never happen.
5. That will never happen.
6. Maybe we'll have time.

Exercise 2

1. What'll
2. It'll
3. Sue'll
4. I'll
5. Where'll
6. He'll

7. she'll
8. That'll

Exercise 6

1. Your table is ready.
2. This headache's getting worse.
3. Maybe, but I'm not sure.
4. Sue is running late.
5. Those're made in Denmark.
6. That's an interesting idea.
7. They might be over there.
8. We were done before you.
9. Bob's certainly acting strange.
10. I think it's done in ink.

Exercise 7

1. one's
2. They're/there
3. I'm
4. You're
5. car's
6. Bill's
7. We're
8. Pat's

Exercise 11

1. Bob's studied English for a while.
2. I would have waited for you.
3. You must have looked a little nervous.
4. What've you done now?
5. What'd you mean?
6. That restaurant's known for its steaks.
7. What's she want?
8. You could have (*coulda*) done more.

Exercise 12

1. What've you
2. Who've they
3. When've I
4. How'd you
5. Why've we
6. Where've we
7. Where's it
8. How've you

Exercise 13

1. How'd the test go?
2. Why'd that happen?
3. Where's this belong?
4. What'd the weather report say?
5. Why'd you do it over?
6. Who's she mean?

Exercise 17

1. It'd be better with more salt.
2. I'd be better prepared next time if I were you.
3. He'd tried to enroll in the class.
4. It had been expected.
5. What'd been done up to that point?
6. How would I have known?
7. We had done that earlier.
8. What could have been done?

Exercise 18

1. I'd go if you'd go.
2. If only we'd found out earlier.
3. Who'd have thought that?

4. They'd considered it for a while.
5. That'd be a good topic for the meeting.
6. That'd seemed like a waste of time.

Exercise 19

1. That'd
2. What'd
3. What'd
4. Dave'd
5. It'd
6. you'd/I'd